DESCENT FROM THE CROSS
TRANSFORMATION OF
A MASOCHISTIC WOMAN

DESCENT
FROM THE
CROSS

TRANSFORMATION OF
A MASOCHISTIC WOMAN

Elaine Simard LaForêt

First Printing, 2024
ISBN 978-0-6451039-5-3

Ordo Templi Orientis

GPO Box 1936
Adelaide, SA 5001
AUSTRALIA

Every effort has been made to determine the ownership of all photos
and secure proper permissions. If any errors have inadvertently occurred,
we apologise and will correct such in subsequent printings.

www.otoaustralia.org.au

Editor: Brendan Walls
Cover Design: Annette Eustace Gray @luxlovesnox_design
Layout: Annette Eustace Gray @luxlovesnox_design

CONTENTS

I dedicate this piece of writing to all my teachers, with special gratitude to three analysts, Edward C. Whitmont, Nathan Schwartz-Salant and Jonathan Goldberg; my three children - Erin, Tara & Gael; nine tenaciously supportive friends - David Dressler, Alice O. Howell, Alexandra Krithades, Daniel McCulloch, Nan Merrill, Joseph Page, Sherry Salman-Brown, Laurie Schapira, and Edith Wallace; Joseph P. Wagenseller, Jungian supervisor, a man of spacious psyche who respected my way even where it differed from his; and each and every analysand whose life I have been privileged to share.

ELAINE LaForêt

JUNG: "My life is the story of the
             self-realization of the unconsciousness.
             Everything in
             the unconscious seeks outward
             manifestation."

"I's" Poem: If I do not draw
             from the well of the unconscious,
             it will draw from me:
             Shall I choose to be drained,
             or, like Egypt's earth,
             yearly silted by the Nile's inundation,
          Shall I choose to be fertilized?

By Virtue of
the Creation,
and still more
of the Incarnation,
nothing here below
is profane
for
those who
know how to see

— Pierre Teilhard de Chardin

PREFACE

Despite encouragement from her supervisors and fellow students at the Jung Institute, Elaine never sought publication for her thesis. She told me she viewed it then as little more than a *by-product* of the processes of psychic transformation it chronicles. Once it was completed, submitted and had allowed her to graduate, she was singularly focused on integrating the hard-won lessons of that psychic transformation and assisting other people at similar points of crisis in a therapeutic context.

Over many years, my enthusiasm for her ideas and work led her to consider publishing it. It wasn't until her health rapidly declined in late 2023 that the idea became a serious focus for her. I then vowed to ensure that her legacy would be preserved for readers and seekers well beyond her remaining time on earth. On lucid days when her strength returned, I received specific instructions from her about her desires for the book you are now holding. Tara, Elaine's beloved daughter, found the typescript of the thesis and the many images and notes related to it. As editor, I have taken all pains to ensure fidelity to that final version, down to the unique formatting of her poems and dream recollections. The only deviation from the academic format of the thesis submission is that I moved endnotes to footnotes, and integrated the many plates, images and figures into the body of the text rather than at the end of the paper. This is in service to the reader and in no way alters the content of this remarkable work.

Editing, design, layout and production of the book was rapid. Everyone involved wanted Elaine to hold a copy of the book while she was still with us. As a result, my attention to detail at times might have been lacking. I take responsibility for this and will ensure that any mistakes that may have occurred during the white heat of this production are corrected in future printings.

Despite our efforts, Elaine died on the 19th of February 2024 without having the opportunity to see the final version. She took some consolation in knowing that it would soon be published.

I'd like to thank Tara for her tireless efforts, in the face of incredible challenges, in making this publication possible, and the small army of supportive friends who ensured that Elaine's final days were filled with love and companionship.

BRENDAN WALLS

Foreword

I had the wonderful fortune to meet Elaine when I began the training program at the CG Jung Institute of New York in 1980. Elaine was a year ahead of me.

We became fast friends, and saw each other through many life difficulties and joys. Elaine was and is a singularly devoted exceptionally loving friend.

In this thesis, written to satisfy a requirement to complete the training program, Elaine takes the extraordinary step to present her own psychological process to her readers. She does this painstakingly, offering dreams, poetry, and a cornucopia of what Jungians call 'amplifications', of archetypal material from the mythologies of the world.

What a symbolic feast this thesis is! But what is so striking is the courage to present her own psyche's journey.

Elaine is a profoundly gifted creative individual born into a family of rigid hierarchy, incapable of seeing the wonderful individual who they had birthed. She was beaten by her punitive father and made to raise the other children in the family because she was the oldest child, thus robbing her of her chance to just be a child.

Like many gifted, creative, and deeply misunderstood and mis-nurtured individuals, particularly women, Elaine suffered to claim her true self from the strictures of the family and the society at the time.

This thesis is the profoundly creative meaningful description of the journey of self-reclamation that she took.

Everyone who came into Elaine's care as a patient, or into her love as a friend are blessed that she undertook this difficult work.

ALEXANDRA KRITHADES, MA, LP
Jungian Psychoanalyst and
President of the CG Jung Institute of New York,
2018-2021

Wilton Connecticut
February 10, 2024

DESCENT
FROM THE
CROSS

TRANSFORMATION OF
A MASOCHISTIC WOMAN

Elaine Simard LaForêt

I

INTRODUCTION

In this paper I will circumambulate aspects of a masochistic process in a woman's psyche, revealing a way of salvation beyond self-immolation. As a prelude to the delineation of a transformation process in the heroine called "I", I will present the anti-heroine of Hawthorne's story "The Birthmark,"[1] the prototype of a life structured masochistically around patriarchal perfectionistic idealization and animus domination. Annihilation of her unique vital creative being, not transformation, is the inevitable finale.

Redeeming masochistic elements involves a woman in experiencing and dismantling the father and mother complexes through which she extracts her true self. The Genesis place for this woman is a territory where she is overwhelmed, externally and internally, by the yang father force; simultaneously, she is alienated from her feminine yin self by a defective relationship to her mother and the Goddess.

Historically, in her response to masculine power, woman has either submitted to male imperatives or defected. She has had to choose between being responsive to a man or responsive to her self, antithetical ways of being that undergird the conflict of the opposites, male and female. Lilith was a woman

---

1   Hawthorne, Nathaniel. *The Complete Novels and Selected Tales*, "The Birthmark," Random House, 1937.

who courageously defected. She abandoned Adam when he demanded total subservience in "the matrimonial position"; he would not accept a non-hierarchical, organic, relational structure in which "on top" and "beneath" revolve like a wheel. Lilith's desire for equality was considered presumptuous, her feminine nature defective; thus, she chose to ostracize herself to the wilderness, where she nursed feelings of alienation and revenge.

Masochistic scarring of women's psyches has been exacerbated for 2,000 years by two archetypal Christian dominants supported by the patriarchal Church Fathers: Christ on the Cross (the martyr animus dying as a service to humanity) and his mother, the Virgin Mary (an unsullied, malleable, all-light woman, split off from the "dark" feminine). By identifying with Christ as crucified Savior in order to balance her experience of man as destructive dominator, woman has fallen from her passion and power into a suicidal repression of her potentiated self. In this paper, I will examine a new masculine animus force represented by the Christ-Dionysus God-expression and accompanying symbols of the balanced cross as opposed to the crucifixion cross, and the standing fish as opposed to the horizontal fish. I will attempt to vivify forces now dead and dying to effect reparation of what was split *asunder*: woman *can* move from martyrdom to her own self-expression, as the sun comes to shine in psyche's dark depths. Heaven on Earth is realized when Earth is no longer seen as a way-station to be suffered in anticipation of future spiritual joy in Heaven. The Dance of Life in the *present* resumes with the infusion of new consciousness.

What dark factors consign women to this dismal trek? How are they psychologically conditioned to a path so alien to their birthright, so distant from fruitful self-development? How come this sundered connection to Isis, to images of power and viability, to affirmation rather than negation of who and what woman is? She has succumbed to doubt, fearfulness and self-judgment. Where is ecstasy, the dance of joy in being, the rebel in self-connection that is also connection to the Self, the god-goddess within? Women have stood ostracized from that great "I am that I am" union, as they strain to conform to the ruling patriarchal psychic and collective constellation. Deaf ears and blind eyes have nullified internalization of the new dispensation manifested in Jesus, the Christ, who is the symbol of a new masculinity come to heal the ravages of the old. The Church converted much of the lived message of the Teacher into structure and stricture, maintaining the transmission of *power over* and domination *in place of a* Way based on the *power of love* and respect for all, a shared journey within each being and among all beings.

The story of "I" is an archeological psychic dig that un-earths an old paradigm of "the feminine experience" and cre-ates a new one: it is the tale of a "sufferer" who learns to walk the way of a "lover". The ongoing "battle of the sexes," strug-gling to be resolved to harmonious interaction, will be unrav-eled. I will attend both to intrapsychic dynamics of masculine and feminine energies-deities and their concomitant outer man-ifestations. The stories are parables, speaking to inner and out-er levels of reality simultaneously, for both landscapes are one.

II

"THE BIRTHMARK": A MODEL OF MASOCHISM NOT TRANSFORMED

In "The Birthmark," Hawthorne recounts the tale of a woman gifted of form, mind and heart, "Queen of her gender," graced with the love in marriage of a most prominent gentleman and scholar, an academic wedded to ideals of perfectibility. Aylmer cannot accept that Georgiana has a birthmark on her cheek and takes it to be "the visible mark of earthly imperfection, ... the symbol of his wife's liability to sin, sorrow, decay, and death."

Fixation on the birthmark starts to erode Aylmer's experience of her goodness and his love. She appears blighted, unacceptable as something less than "ideal loveliness." He is unable to accept that anything born into Reality from the world of Form is marked by Nature:

> "...Seeing her otherwise so perfect, he found this one defect grow more and more intolerable with every moment of their united lives. It was the fatal flaw of Humanity which Nature, in one shape or another, stamps ineffaceably on all her productions."[1]

---

1   ibid, pg. 1022.

In the East, a flaw is actually *imposed* on a piece of art to indicate it is human, not ethereal and ideal; no crystal is perfect, either. Furthermore, in the East, the flaw is considered the agent of "perfection," a representation of wholeness resulting from the union of the opposites of perfect and imperfect. Aylmer's mind and heart, sculpted by Western and Christian thought-forms tyrannized by an inner demand for perfection, projects this value onto the Beloved Woman. Focusing more and more on her "flaw," he finds himself in an oppositional relationship to Nature — God, whom he deems responsible for his affliction. Aylmer is bent on enabling his woman to meet his idealized image of the feminine, compensating once and for all for 'evil Eve'. He has no understanding of incarnational processes and the human condition that include such mundanity as "muling and puking in the nurse's arms..."[2] A soul human-born is no longer wrapped in heaven's luminous garments trailing gossamer threads of beauty.

Finally, Aylmer offers to use his scientific expertise to remove her birthmark. He is inflated with the idea of correcting Nature and believes it is his calling to rectify God's divine manifestation in the feminine form, thereby enabling her to be perfect here on earth and perfectly lovable as well.

After initial protestations at his judgment of her mark and a questioning of his evaluation, Georgiana submits to Aylmer's proposal to improve her nature. She is unable to risk the withdrawal of his love and cannot bear his painful disapproval. Without an internalized autonomous sense of her own worth, she feels devoid of meaning. Furthermore, she is infected with his enthusiasm for her perfection: he says,

---

2   Shakespeare, William. *As You Like It*, Act II, scene 7.

> "Fear not, dearest! ... Do not shrink from me! Believe me, Georgiana, I even rejoice in this single imperfection, since it will be such a rapture to remove it."[3]

Given Georgiana's seduction by the possibility of being without flaw and given her psychological dependence on positive mirroring by the masculine, she is driven between Scylla and Charybdis, the rock and the whirlpool. Will she crash into the abyss of nothingness represented by his withdrawing of approval, the very source of her being, or, will she drown in the abyss of non-being by sacrificing her God-given form to his manipulative ministrations, cloaked as they are in the casuistry of self- transformation ideals? Impotent to claim her identity as valuable and viable as she is, she acquiesces to Aylmer's desire and drinks his "healing" potion. A woman without roots in her own ground, her earthbody, she cannot hold sway against winds that blow from her Beloved Man. Georgiana's submission is not that of a firmly rooted personal self who seeks to connect to what will be self-creating, but of one overwhelmed by a masculine idealized self-expectation. Only too late, as she is leaving her body, the soul's cord to incarnate mortal life having been severed through the removal of the birthmark, does she start to realize her collusion with the male ideal of the "peerless bride":

> "My poor Aylmer," she repeated, with a more than human tenderness, "you have aimed loftily; you have done nobly. Do not repent that with so high and pure a feeling, you have rejected the best the earth could offer. Aylmer, dearest Aylmer, I am dying!"[4]

---

3   Hawthorne, *Op Cit.*, p. 1026.
4   Ibid., p. 1032.

The "now perfect woman" goes to the only suitable abode for flawless ones, as her soul takes "its heavenward flight." It is an extraordinary revelation of a woman's self-projection onto a man that even in her dying, she relates totally to him, with no "I am" except for, "I am dying."

This story exposes the curse under which woman has labored "to be in His-Image" for aeons. She has stayed stuck in an ego-ideal with no access to her true self and Source.[5] A man who understands once said, "To love only perfection is just another way of hating life, for life is not perfect." Woman's development has been radically stunted by a splitting off from much of what has been categorized as "shadow," i.e., whatever facets of womanhood challenge the domination of patriarchal values and would imbue her with power if she connected to them: authoritativeness, assertiveness, insurgence, chaos, felt-knowing, irrationality, passion, her *own* need and desire, selfishness, and self-relatedness, to list a few.

Deviation from His-Expectation is experienced as a danger that alienates woman from the much-sought benediction of the fathers, and the successful splitting off of "undesirable" attributes allows entrance into male inner sanctums. The more acquiescent, other-oriented, "giving and nice" a woman is, the more she is valued and feels herself viable. Her submission to the masculine is not in the service of her self, hence not life-giving, but rather a sacrificial offering of what she has not yet claimed - her own substance and soul. This kind of submission executes a death-blow to any possibility of self-emergence. These women live a death-in-life, their egos bonded to an animus in whom is vested all power and authority. Feminine being, expressed through self-abnegation and self-sacrifice, is

---

5   See also Woodman, Marion. *Addiction to Perfection*, Inner City Books, 1982, for additional material on woman's struggle for perfected being.

consumed by the masculine force. She is a piggy-back woman, feet off the ground, bereft and homeless.

Meanwhile, her negative repressed feelings, all the hate, anger, and frustration of one in servitude, are inflicted on her own exiled self, as she wanders in the wasteland of ego images that revolve around face lifts, breast lifts, "the Good, the True and the Beautiful." She is up-lifted, dried out, without access to black earth and turquoise waters within her essential nature, which longs to become vested in its Source - the Goddess archetype of Feminine Holy-Wholeness.

What process of conscious evolution is required for Hawthorne's heroine to transform her masochism, her fateful surrender in a death-marriage to the greedy perfectionistic animus that refuses to embrace the human shadow?

The masochistic martyr woman in the West has received inspiration and confirmation from images of Christianity, particularly Jesus suffering at Gethsemane and the Christ crucified on the Cross. Why were these particular facets of Christ's life singled out for emphasis? Why his Passion and Death, not his Resurrection? Why suffering-martyrdom, and not joy and rebirth, an affirmation of the soul's ongoing life? Woman's resonance with the crucified Christ has been an unconscious alliance of victims, while the Church Fathers' emphasis on the symbol of the Crucifix has kept the "religious" population continually aware of their sinful vulnerability and consequent dependency on the Church for salvation. Even today, the church liturgy throughout the year emphasizes crucifixion with a minimal response to resurrection teachings of new life. Matthew Fox, a Dominican priest whose teachings emphasize the Cosmic Christ and the God-seed alive in everyone, has been silenced by the Church. Teilhard de Chardin, another Christian mystic, who like Eckhart saw God in all things and all things in God, a life-affirming view, was able to be published only posthumously.

Georgiana of "The Birthmark" was a woman who colluded with the crucifixion of her soul-self in the service of self-definition *vis 'a vis* the other, devoid of any conscious relationship to her self. Her self-sense was contingent upon meeting a prescribed image. As a venerated dominated object, she rested on her laurels in a simulated victory that denied *any* emergence of Feminine Wholeness. Intolerant judgment of her nature displaced a reverential attitude toward woman as Nature's creation.

What actually needed to be crucified for self-creative evolution was her identification with patriarchal values through a claiming of her own value. Georgiana might have said, "My birthmark is ME, my unique individual sign! If you can't accept it, we will have to part."

III

"I": A Process of
Masochism Transforming

"I": THE FATHER AND MOTHER COMPLEXES

This section involves the introduction of another patriarchal-daughter heroine, a composite of the analyst and her female analysands, whose entanglement with the masculine leads not to love-death but to love-life. This animus-identified martyr woman, unlike Georgiana, frees herself from male domination to experience connection to her self and fruitful interaction with an Eros-infused masculine principle. Exploring this patriarchal daughter's relationship to her father and to the masculine principle inevitably precipitates looking at the mother-daughter constellation. Both will be woven together in a circumambulation around the complexes. Hillman wrote:

> "Our complexes are history at work in the soul; it is so much easier to transcend history by climbing the mountain and let come what may than it is to work on history within us, our reactions, habits, moralities. ... Change in the valley requires recognition of history, an archaeology of the soul, a digging in the ruins, a re-collecting."[1]

---

1   Hillman, James. "Peaks and Vales," *Puer Papers*, Spring Publication, University of Dallas, 1979, p.67.

The composite heroine, whom I shall call "I," came into her life as a "father's daughter", physically birthed from her mother's womb, but psychically bonded to her father, who switched his allegiance (anima projection) from her mother to her at birth. Psychologically this father-connection is a precursor to her patriarchal bondage. This father's daughter came to experience her unrelenting inner attachment to remaining "maiden," unavailable for masculine penetration and a journey into the underworld depths of her psyche.[2] She felt hurt when her analyst in the first stages of her analysis referred to her "virgin" complex, not knowing then that remaining maiden was a psychic chastity belt protecting against further incursions of the masculine, as well as maintaining her father's dominion over her.[3]

Looking further at this composite heroine, we see her crucified on the vertical pole of the fathers. The tree in the following dream, like the Christian crucifix, expresses life-distorted, in both cases with an over-abundance of yang energy moving upward away from earth and life. To heal this *unnatural* configuration of the tree within her core self, "I" began Jungian analysis. It is revealed in the dream that her true nature can only be made available through a radical truncating of the hypertrophic tree (an image of identification with the phallos) and an extensive exploration of many repressed contents: a *process* must take place to recover and rectify her authentic being:

---

2   For further amplification of "maiden" archetypal and psychological dynamics, refer to Kerenye's article "Kore" in *Essays on a Science of Mythology*, Bollingen Series XXII, Princeton University Press, 1973.

3   These themes are elaborated in the fairy tale "The Handless Maiden" and in *The Woman Sealed in the Tower* by Betsy Caprio, Paulist Press, N.Y., 1982.

A man is axing a huge tree, no ordinary tree this one shoot-
ing hundreds of feet up. The trunk without branches goes up
many feet; the center section is loaded with stark, unleafed,
asymmetrical branches; the top section is pure trunk again,
ending bluntly way up in the sky. I am aghast that the man is
cutting down such a unique giant. He surprises me, however,
by revealing that he knows how to cut off just the top by cutting into the bottom a certain way. He is making a triangular
incision; when the two lines meet in the trunk, the top will
fall, he says. I watch. Finally, the top cracks off and begins
to fall through the air: I move carefully so that it won't land
on me. It lands a short distance away. I go to investigate and
discover that the tree has smashed into the middle of a ceme-
tery, sending tombstones flying into the road on either side. I
am worried about what has happened, because I realize there
is no way to figure out which tombstone goes with which
coffin. Digging in to find the bodies won't help because the
dead reduced to bones cannot be recognized and reconnected
with their names on the tombstones.

The dream guided "I" to excavate a particular archetypal
manifestation of the ambivalent mother archetype in her psyche. What follows is a part of her travail with the mother complex.

Jung's discussion of the intermediate type of mother complex, which he terms "Resistance to the Mother," flooded her
with insight into her own psychology. Her mother's devotion
to the role of good Catholic wife and mother — ever present,
ever giving, ever fertile, ever subservient to her husband, "I's"
father — triggered a resolution *never to be like her*, never to
be without an autonomous existence, without a connection to
the wider worlds of relationship, intellect, and numinosity. "I"
knew she did not want to be homebody, except in a minor
way, maybe, someday. Incontrovertibly the object of a negative

mother complex, "I" wrote a poem about the psychic bondage
to her mother's way:

Strangulation

The cord of my complex
stunts my breath
as I struggle to be born,
thwarts my blood, my body,
from surging into life...

lifeless, "anything-but" daughter,
cut off from roots and womb,
a stranger to her self...

How can I dance, twist, insist,
unravel this cursed rope,
to grope my way to bliss?

Life, however, had other ideas. Of this kind of woman,
Jung says, "...or else a diabolical fate will present her with a
husband who shares all the essential traits of her mother's character."[4] So it was. But fate didn't stop there: in spite of herself,
or because of herself, having been taken over by an unremitting
pressure to have a child, "I" had stopped working and by the
time of the dream had been imprisoned in domesticity for seven
years with three small children, two adopted and one unex-
pectedly natural. Maternal duties were unbearable, marital life
deficient. Jung continues, "Because of her merely unconscious

---

4   Jung, Carl Gustav., "Psychological Aspects of the Mother Archetype."
The Archetypes and the Collective Unconscious, Vol 9. 1, Princeton University Press, 1977, p. 91.

reactive attitude toward reality, her vessel to serve a man and children, life actually becomes dominated by what she fought hardest against - the exclusively maternal feminine aspect."[5] He adds that the way to overcome this negative mother complex, any complex in fact, is to suffer it to the full, drink down to the very dregs what we have averted ourselves from. "I" was truly in the dregs, sunk in the maternal womb and very unconscious of the nature of her condition, at the time of the dream.

"I" experienced powerful affects around this dream - affects engendered by the act of cutting which she, feeling identified with the tree, experienced as a wounding in the generative area. In actuality, a year before, "I" had been under medical pressure to have her womb severed from her body. And she felt great dis-ease at the upheaval in the graveyard, for the disarray and chaos were so unsettling to her rational mind.

For a long time, "I" agonized over the inner horrors of dismemberment and disorder. What pain would she have to suffer in her feminine core to be made well? Rooted in "I's" psyche was a tree that would have to be chopped out in the womb area to rehabilitate it. For weeks after the dream, "I" wandered through the hours of her daily life, tearful, feeling a tearing, wrenching in her guts. She knew, as the man had told her, that the wounding would bring healing, but that did not assuage the pain. She was to learn that only a deep process of self-examination could guide her through the pain to joy. These affects were paramount in her beginning analysis. Seven years later, "I" wrote the following poems out of experiences prefigured by the dream:

---

5   Ibid., p.99.

(1) I surrendered to his scalpel
         In the antiseptic darkness,
              he came,
                   Hades,
         to open my womb,
         ripping out fruitless foetuses.

yet not enough:
              into the vagina, he eased himself,
              gently, painlessly, he penetrated again —
              to cleanse and purify.

still not enough:
              my bladder he punctured
                   that I might pour forth -
                   no more holding back,
              no more containment and concealment...

Eros, did you mean to penetrate my heart,
              to shoot your arrow there?
         Why did you miss your mark,
              your scalpel gone awry?
         Deny me not the knowing:
              cross the threshold
                   with your gift
                   please, no sudden thrift
                   after such extravagance

(2) May 14, 1985 London

> Uroboric uterus
> feasting on my flesh
>   creating vessels
>   for your own bloody sustenance,
>   propagating fibroids
>   masquerading as fetuses.
>
> Womb playground of secret mother,
>   suckling herself:
>   I could not turn my back on Her—
>   She *will* hold sway,
>   If not through nature straight,
>   She fecundates
>   in her own dark way.

In reading Jung's material and Neumann's on the Mother Archetype, "I" was thrust headlong back for another encounter with these images. Neumann writes in *The Great Mother*:

> The center of this vegetative symbolism of the Great Earth Mother who brings forth all life from herself is the tree. As fruit-bearing tree of life, it is female: it bears, transforms, nourishes; its leaves, branches, twigs are "contained" in it and dependent on it. The protective character is evident in the treetop that shelters nests and birds. But in addition the tree trunk is a container, "in" which dwells its spirit, as the soul dwells in the body. The female nature of the tree is demonstrated in the fact that treetops and trunk can give birth, as in the case of Adonis and many others.[6]

---

6   Neumann, Erich. *The Great Mother*, Princeton University Press, Princeton, NJ, 1974, pp. 48-49.

The tree, as a symbol of the Great Mother, includes also the male principle, not yet separated out, but part of her uroboric all-in-oneness.

So, although her personal experience of mother led on one level to a rejection of the maternal, the primordial maternal, imaged in this great tree, still moves in and through her. Going now beyond the affects, "I" looked more closely at the nature of the tree as it appeared in her dream: it is hypertrophic, it has grown unnaturally, for energy has gone not into leaves and fruit, but rather into a second phallic trunk that does not belong there. Maternal energy has flowed into a sky-reaching, upward-thrusting masculine spirit momentum that robs the feminine-maternal of its generative and nutritive potentialities. On the other hand, the tree is powerfully vital, but wrong, too much: it is a real "fucking mother," assertive and overbearing, yin and yang radically out of balance.

"I" feels in the dream as if the male cutting the tree is not valuing it; he is destroying the tree, raping *mater materia*. He tells her, however, that he knows how to heal its abortive growth, and, in fact, only the top falls off. His act, "I" came to see, confirms the human capacity for consciousness and intentionality to intervene in the Great Mother's nature's, the unconscious'- inexorable process of growth; it is possible to trim the Great Tree when it grows awry: that is, to rework, recreate, and create one's being, physically and psychologically. The pillar part of the tree must be brought back to earth. Through its removal, "her" energy can return from its phallic-animus digression (rerouting) to the roots, to *Her body*, and begin to form leaves and fruit, bringing protection and nourishment. In fact, Neumann, in *The Great Mother* writes:

Transformation symbolism becomes sacral where, over and above the purely natural transformative process, there is an intervention by men; where it ceases to be a process only of nature or the unconscious and the human personality enters into it and heightens it.[7]

As "I" re-experienced this dream, she came to know that the tree chopper was not a devil's minion but a true tree-doctor, the perpetrator of the necessary healing wound: a careful triangular incision representing the incursion of consciousness into the chaos of the maternal womb - the place of generativity - that had birthed a misplaced phallic appendage. The unnatural symbiosis of the phallus and the mother must be broken if masculine insemination is to occur in creative form as spirit that infuses her feminine nature, instead of sapping it.

This radical separation of the superfluous trunk brings about upheaval in the graveyard. The first transformation in the realm of the Mother — the tree - leads to ever greater possibilities for consciousness as wood coffins (emblems of the Mother as the shelterer of the dead, the mother of death) pop up out of earth's dark embrace. Repressed contents, previously served by the negative animus represented by the trunk, are thrust up from the depths of the unconscious into the daylight world of consciousness. Like Psyche, "I" has been presented with a sorting project of rather large proportions, which requires skills of differentiation not yet utilized to retrieve aspects of her self heretofore sealed in the womb of the terrible mother of unconsciousness, who "draws the life of the individual back into herself ." Breaking the thrall of the mother complex may bring to light parts of the psyche consigned to death because of unavailable energy.

---

7   Ibid., p.59.

At the dream's end "I", looking at the chaos of coffins and trying to figure out how to reorganize them, stood with her back to the trimmed tree. She was to learn in the years that followed how she served the masculine principle and the negative mother, not her own nature. The dream experience was a summons not to turn her back on a new symmetry, on her personal tree-self, as her own maternal-nature and much femininity had been given over in projection to her personal mother.

Instead, "I" could consciously allow Her - the Goddess presence - to affect, not afflict, her with fruitful power and potential.

The status of "I's" relationship to the masculine was further suggested in a dream she had six months later, shortly after beginning analysis:

I am at a big gathering at a hotel with people, groups everywhere. First, I misplace my canvas bag with clothes and such, then my purse. I search everywhere, up and down elevators and escalators. I'm waiting for a man friend to pick me up. Then, there's a huge fire or explosion and the place must be completely vacated. We all go helter-skelter onto the street.

Now, I'm inside a cavernous building laced with stair wells, metal stairs suspended in air. Suddenly, I am confronted by two tough, young, sweet-faced, empty-eyed Adonis-type men; they come toward me to rape me. I push away and start running; they follow. Somehow, I dispense with one, the second still chases. I turn to face him, as a group of people appear below. I shout for help, but they stare blankly. At this point, I strike at the young man with a pair of fingernail scissors, puncturing him in the temple and cheek. He collapses dead. I cringe with horror at how it felt to plunge into his flesh, but I am also hugely relieved.

When her analyst appeared horrified and suggested there were possibilities other than destruction of the attackers, "I" was appalled. For her there seemed no other way — she had felt so threatened by what she perceived as possible violation and annihilation. When "I" left that day, she wondered whether she should return to pursue a process that seemed so deficient in understanding and that left her feeling vulnerable, defenseless, and guarded.

Later, after much brooding, "I" returned to this dream and was able to find support for this violent behavior as compensation for her naive openness to immature, unconscious men, i.e., son-lover types wanting maternal nurturance and mirroring. Her psyche in the dream gathered enough strength to prevent this animus from taking her over internally. The dream experience provided an intimation of energy becoming available, if she could become conscious, for her to take a stance against the power of sexuality continuing to lead her into unsatisfactory subservient relationships. Identified with providing warmth and resonance for men, "I" at that time, needed an infusion of ruthlessness from the unconscious psyche for self-protection.

At that point in "I's" journey, the internal feminine-Persephone was still the maiden bound to the Demeter-mother. Of that, she was totally unaware. Hades, the facilitator for a connection to the feminine depths, was to be resisted at all costs. "Going down and getting wet" - essential directions and modalities for the self-journey — were anathema to her; the path was high and dry, a movement toward masculine spirit without soul, disembodied or, as Hillman would say, movement toward the peaks leaving the vales behind - and, in "I's" case, not knowing there were vales to be dwelt in at all.

Back to "her" story: What was it that set "I" in opposition to the masculine function, so that the masculine she needed for her own development became an adversary? What formed the obstacles that would not allow surrender? For initiation into the depths requires, above all, surrender, the closing of the eyes and the entry into darkness which, as Kerenyi notes, is something active. He says further, "The passivity of Persephone, of the bride, the maiden doomed to die, is re-experienced by means of an *inner act* - if only an act of surrender."[8] ONLY an act of surrender !!!

For "I", the act of surrendering ("to put under") had been rendered terrifying, associated with going UNDER, being lost, more specifically, being a slave to her father's will - to a dominating patriarchal ethos which he embodied in action and attitude, and even articulated with such statements as "My word is law," to which her mother responded submissively, "Thy will be done." As the oldest of six children, "I" was expected "to tow the line" - to follow her father's demands for hard work, rigid Catholic morality, superior performance everywhere. What's more, *he* was to be revered, respected, and never questioned. If "I" chanced to question his values or to criticize his harshness, she was severely reprimanded, even beaten. For protection from his tyranny, most of what "I" felt and thought went into hiding, a secret resistance and self-withholding, while on the surface she seemed available. This many-faceted resistance involved remaining staunchly maiden (i.e., internally not surrendering), thus attracting masculine veneration, and/or challenge. She also found safety in playing mother to men, all of which enabled her to preserve herself intact in a glass mountain, a girl afraid of being born into womanhood:

> You bypass my heart
> in the great glass bower -
> No blessed cracks
> for my breath to start,
> the wrong gate is breached
> deflowered again

---

8   Kerenyi, Carl. *Dionysus*, Princeton University Press, Princeton, 1976.

    yet virgin-hearted
    penetration without creation
    pregnancy without birth.

  I yearn
    for the right wound,
    for your trek
    across the Great Divide
    to torch my frozen soul.

  At last...
You brave the icy silence, hidden pride,
    the fierce terrain,
    the no-man's land
      where terrors reign...

  Still, I stand
    a target ready for rupture,
    as arrow upon arrow
      crosses the chasm,

  quickening
    my hibernating heart,
    bull's eyes everywhere,
    watching your resonant voice
    stream across the barren earth
      redeeming the rape
      from the long illusion
  the earth quakes
  my cup runneth over,
    life, once a dream,
      erupts into living.

What "I" did not become conscious of until much later was that undergirding her refusal to surrender was her unconscious pre-existent surrender dictated not just by her father experience but by the dominant mythologem in the collective unconscious: Christ as the One Who Surrenders. Endowed with vitality by the Christian Church and especially by women in their assumption of a secondary role to men, this mythologem had been carefully programmed into "I's" unconscious. (She had also been taught a Creation Story in which Adam was created *First* in God's own image, Eve *Second* from Adam, and not God, AND out of one of his ribs — a relatively insignificant body part!) What "I" became aware of was that, in fact, her core self had surrendered unconsciously to patriarchal ideation "centuries" ago: a submission unlike that taught in the ancient Mysteries wherein the submission of the psyche to death is in expectation of transformation. For two thousand years, the Western world has experienced a standstill of the Mysteries through a fixation on the Christ of Surrender-Crucifixion-Death. This surrender has lost its link in ritual as a prerequisite for resurrection, relegating to the unconscious a sense of cycle, of feminine organic evolving time, and of rebirth. Would it be possible to surrender creatively the ego to the Self and thus redeem the Christ within from his paralysis on the Cross of Death? In order for "I" to retrieve the essence and reality of the true Christ as a model for the individuation process, she must re-integrate into consciousness the image of Christ living, dying *and* resurrecting.

An aspect of non-surrender "I" had not recognized before was that her connection to her mother fostered a stance of invisible invulnerability - a feeling of safety in her mother's domain that preempted the journey to the underworld of her own depths and desires; for that journey would involve separating from the mother-world and finding her own self-syntonic way. Originally, if anyone asked "I" about her mother, "I" would assuredly say, "She is a perfect mother." After all, she had dedicated herself to the hearth, always there at home singing a cheery song. Mother didn't mind that she had given up social life, freedom, spontaneity, to be total mother and wife - perfectly acquiescent to her fate. "I" didn't realize the extent of her unconscious link to her mother, since she was primarily aware of the strength of her resistance. Like her mother, "I" came to see that she expected herself to be happily accepting of her lot — the contented martyr — and her lot was to be motherhood and servility. So, while on one level "I" was raging against feminine stereotypes, on the other hand, "I" accepted her values. She even pleased her mother by marrying a man similar to her mother (the opposite of her dominating father) and deluding herself that she had escaped submission to mother's way by traveling, being a professional woman, and deciding to put off having children.

So, "I's" main experience of the feminine through her mother was that being a woman involved abandoning herself in service to a man, sacrificing independence, relatedness and real *joie de vivre*. "I" determined never to be like her, never to submit. Gradually, through the process of becoming self-aware, "I" differentiated the issue of submission and surrender.

When she was reading about the Mysteries at Eleusis, "I" heard a dark voice announce, "You are excluded from the rites - you have failed to surrender." Then suddenly, she recognized, "I *have* surrendered, but all wrong - I have served my mother's negative sacrifice and have served my father's attitude that as woman I am NOT allowed, I am denied entrance to the Mysteries—I have served the phallus- it has not served me." Two dreams arose to confront "I" with this facet of her self:

Dream One

I am in a room with a man - he lies prone - his distinguishing feature is the size of his cock, the length of the room, a real Gulliver - and I, like Thumbelina, am standing as high as the tip and massaging it with my filmy gown.

Why am I so small? Here I am serving the man and his needs – how insignificant I feel myself to be. I am only significant through pleasing HIM.

Dream Two

I go out to a barn. On a platform in one corner is a huge white cow (four times normal size) in heat and about to be mated. Tied next to her is a young bull. This is his first time. He is all twisted in his rope. I wonder if he'll figure out how to mount her. He turns around several times, managing to extend his rope and plunges into her. As this happens, a sunburst corona silently explodes above them — I am awestruck by this dazzling light circle and know it's the universe's response to the moment of conception.

The animals part, exposing a man behind them who says, "This is none of your business. Get out of here!" I turn silently and slink out. He makes me feel like an intruder.

Seen from one angle, this dream exposes "I's" unconscious expectations of put-downs from men, the patronizing authority figures. Father's voice says, "Who do you think you are?" and pulls the curtain down on the just-witnessed *coniunctio*. The put-downs are revealed to be fully internalized. "'I" is excluded and allows herself to be without protest. Nonetheless, she has seen the mystery, she is a *seer*, although the judgmental animus castigates her as a *voyeur*, criticizing her for partaking of the feast of life in a vision of the numinous. "I" realized that her ego had been propped up with pride in not submitting - adamantly not capitulating - staying high, apart, and condescending. This dream reflected back to her a humiliating awareness of her unconscious servility - a passive submission to patriarchal denigration leading away from her true self, unlike that of true surrender, which could lead to her self.

What "I" *sees* in this dream is what the patriarchal animus is threatened by: for the scenario is an allusion to the matriarchal mysteries with the mother-son lover dynamism. Here the "leashed" submissive male principle *serves* the female, whereas in the Gulliver dream the power roles are reversed in a way palatable to the patriarchal constellation in "I's" psyche. In some matriarchal mysteries, the Goddess empowers herself through the young virile male, using his seed for her fertilization, exactly the opposite of the patriarchal male who fertilizes himself with the female's soul. Both the matriarchal and patriarchal ways thrive on use and exploitation of the opposite sex; interactions are hierarchical and power-based. It is understandable that "I's" dominant animus would try to outcast her from *seeing* the highly potentiated feminine (the great white cow can be seen as a theriomorphic personification of Isis-Hathor) over which the masculine holds no sway, but is only *in service to*. "I" wondered whether she would ever see/experience an inner union of the masculine and feminine principles activated by the power of love, where giving and receiving are one and where there is no urgency to use another, since love is offered freely.

It was through the therapeutics of her analytic process that "I" received validation and understanding of her *inner* experiences: she was *seen* by her analyst and could thus claim her own *seeing*. She began to feel viable, baptized into new life by a personal experience of having someone's "countenance shine upon her":

In the forest of the psyche
>   I have seen the hypertrophic tree,
>   its extra trunk hacked
>>   from its very core —

From the mountain of the soul
>   I have seen the great she-turtle
>   fly up from watery depths
>   to alight on her stony bowl
>>   in the sea—

At the theatre of the spirit
>   I have seen the great white Cow
>   receive upon her altar the virgin bull,
>   crowned by a corona
>>   in the sky—

Today *he saw I saw*,
Blessed my exiled experience.

As indicated earlier, preparation for the journey down to the depths of psyche involves a separating from the mother - Persephone's release from the thrall of Demeter. "I" recalls two dreams reflecting that process: in the first, "I" was bewildered in that she was kicking her mother out of the family home, sending her over the hill. (Remember, at that time she considered her mother perfect...) In the second dream, the following occurred:

> My mother and I are standing at the edge of an old French village built up the side of a rock cliff. Suddenly, she tumbles down a rocky-concrete trough on the side of the hill. She calls out, "I, help me!" but I am immobilized: if I jump after her, I too will be harmed. Fortunately, a man part way down stops

her fall and she climbs back up the trough. At the top, I take her in my lap, hold and rock and comfort her. She is like a little child. I am relieved and amazed to discover she has no bruises from her fall. I check her head carefully.

Suddenly, across the street we see a grey-haired woman maniacally laughing and talking as she smears her car with slogans. It is clear she's psychotic and a crowd gathers. Mother goes over to see and tells me this woman is so happy because she's decided to commit suicide.

Next scene: We hear the woman has committed suicide. She has disposed of everything but her car and bed. Mother and I are trying to decide what to do with them. Then mother tells me she has "decided" too. Staying around any longer is fruitless, she says. She is so determined and "set" that it never occurs to me to try to change her mind. I know there is nothing I can do. She disappears and I'm alone in a house crying and crying and walking from room to room.

At first, "I" is mother to the mother - a replay of what she in fact was but didn't know until the dream unearthed the data. In reality, "I" had had no childhood - only a great deficit in mothering. She mothered her mother and five younger siblings.[9]

"I" wrote a poem expressing her yearning for maternal nurturance:

April, 1984

Secret: the woman will find me wanting:

>   only a vacant place
>   to house the lost waif:

---

9   See Miller, Alice. *The Drama of the Gifted Chld*, for an extended discussion of children without childhood.

      never safe in mother-embrace
      empty spaces
          beg to be seen

      the well is dry
      floods fill the eye
      of this sky daughter
      searching now
          for moist mother.

Through mother's leaving in the dream, "I" is restored to daughter, who only as the maiden can undertake the journey to the underworld. In reality, "I," at the time of the dream, decided to divorce the husband she had married partially to please her mother. When her mother was distressed by the divorce, "I" told her: "*You* have some very heavy things to deal with." Finally, "I" stopped feeling wrong for being different from her mother and choosing her own way.

The second major part of the preparation for the downward way to the depths of "I's" psyche involved a defusing of the masculine force as something to be resisted, bringing in new sense of the masculine as an essential mediator to the core - *kore* - of the feminine self. This transformation was abetted in reality by two important relationships with men. One man was the first to see the terrified, protected girl-child beneath the sure woman: he brought understanding and tenderness. The other was "I's" male analyst, a man both incisive and gentle, with whom she could test her projections of violation and non-acceptance. "I" awaited the sword of Damocles, but found instead acceptance, reflection - and space to move in.

In dreams, young men figures made appearances: one, a youth, Parsifal-like, was pure, open to experience. "I" drank his sperm from a cup. Others, considerate in approach, offered themselves to a body-psyche becoming more available:

I am lying on my back on a bed. Before me appear three strong, naked masculine figures. They stand still, shoulder to shoulder at the foot of the bed, facing me. Not one has a familiar face. They are totally unknown and totally impersonal. Their faces reflect a powerful sureness and centeredness. One speaks: "Which one of us do you want first?" I reply, "All of you." Together they enter me. The whirlwind, a vortex of circulating force, a fruit-filled cornucopia, reaches a crescendo in my totally receptive body.

Why the number three? Emblem of the dynamic masculine energy. Does "I" get the point yet? Self-defense is no longer necessary: this IS surrender, not submission. The masculine force does not come to cut her down, but rather to introduce her to her deepest nature, her womb-self. So does Hades serve Persephone, the maiden. Without him, she would still be cavorting endlessly in sunny fields. "I" accepted the insemination of the masculine; she welcomed what previously was experienced as so intrusive that it was to be resisted with all the energy of a psyche assiduously guarding its virginity.

A readiness to go down and to get wet was at hand - a return to the vale, to Nature. Another dream pointed to a radical shift from the original patriarchal orientation of "I's" psyche; this landmark dream radically altered the inner status quo:

I'm trekking with a companion to reach a castle on a hill where I will meet the lord of the manor. The castle is distant. Under a bright hot sun, we are hiking on and on through field and swamp. Sharp grasses cut my bare legs, my feet keep bogging down in wet areas. Finally, I say I've got to stop a moment. We pause, and I look to my right where I see in the distance, on the other side of the one winding road, a village by the sea. Suddenly, I know that's where I want to go, not the castle. My companion agrees to shift direction in order to visit the village.

When we arrive, we enter through a gateway into a courtyard. There we are greeted by a young man who informs us that his mother, who is apparently the head of the village, will be back soon to speak with us. He tells us that she used to be nervous and exhausted but she is well now, for "daily she walks behind the cows." I look out beyond the village and, as if in a vision, witness a single line of cows processing out along a peninsula of land; slowly, slowly, they move, and slowly behind them walks a young woman, her hair swaying gently back and forth with the rhythm of the procession.

"I" was reminded here of Hillman's discussion of body-consciousness in "On Psychological Femininity." He talks about a body-consciousness that gives a somaticized awareness of self in concrete actual behavior. He elaborates as follows:

> This would in turn transform that old frustration of reflection divided from action, where consciousness is conceived mainly in terms of speech and mind, giving over the unconscious to the body and its "actings-out." The body might no longer be the realm only of abyss and passion; it might now fill up with slowness and interiority.[10]

This image/experience of the cow, which represents the primal principle of humidity, enabled "I" to connect with another kind of feminine energy - ruminative, natural, earthy and lunar: the vegetative consciousness reactions of the psyche. Through the years, this image of a stately, grounded woman, attuned to a cyclical and circular, non-ascending, non-striving movement

---

10   Hillman, James. *The Myth of Analysis*, Harper & Row, NY, 1978, p. 285.

and moment has come to nurture and to quiet ... a reminder that progress is also made by staying in one place, not always hiking heroically upward toward a lofty, fantasied goal.

In Egypt several years later, "I" made further contact with the cow deity (see Plates XXV, XXVI, XXVII, XXVIII). Encountering the Great Goddess Isis in her theriomorphic feral cow form catapulted "I" into an intense experience of the nourishing maternal level missing in her childhood. This animal representation with the sun disk on her head communicated the noble dignity and calm authority of the mother principle, enabling her to claim, finally, the maternal as positive.

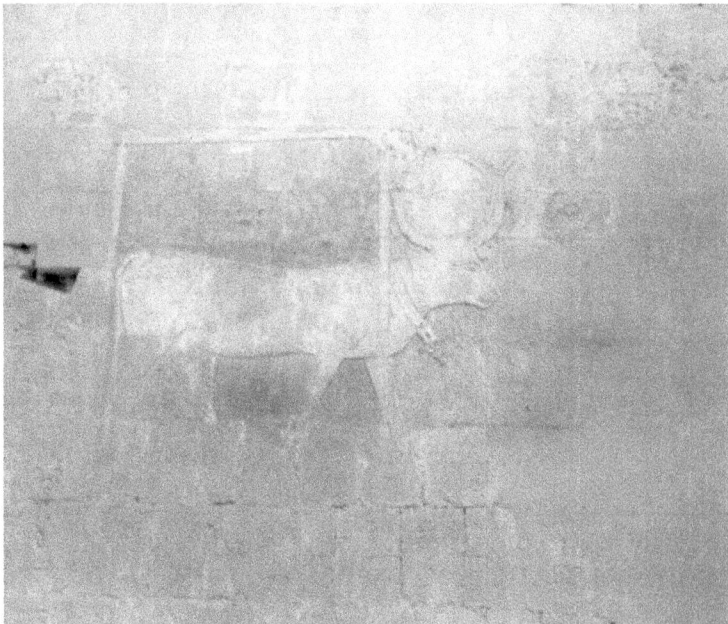

Plate XXV

Plate XXVI

"Daily she walks behind the cows": Interiority is a value much to be desired. As an antidote to "nervous exhaustion" of psychic resources, receptive practice incorporated into the daily round balances active, assertive doing. Thus one is regenerated with healing energy in the process of spending oneself. At the end of his "Psalm of Life," Longfellow wrote:

Let us then be up and doing
With a heart for any fate.
Learn to labor and to wait.

Like a mantra, these lines periodically surface into her consciousness since "I" first read and copied them down at a friend's house when she was in seventh grade. Now she hears, in a conscious way, the final word, "wait", revealing again how much her receptivity has been in the shadow. Pieces of self

Plate XXVII

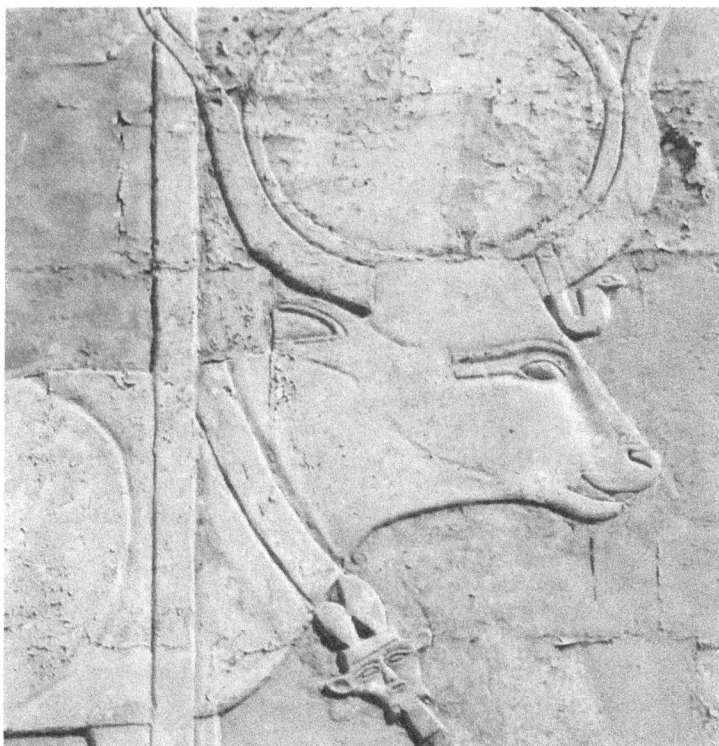

Plate XXVIII

are coalescing: "doing" and "being" pairing within - "Learn to labor and to wait." "I" heeded the call to yield to her receptive bovine nature in order to combine that part of herself with the capacity to assert, with that inner bull pawing the ground these many centuries. "I" realized that she could choose not to abort her feminine self by neglecting the soft yin modalities, while remembering that too much receptivity leads to dullness and too much assertion leads to depletion. Each is not merely complement, but also balm for the other. At this time "I" wrote for her self a small poem:

Be as the tea -
        allow yourself to steep
        these are deep matters
        that cannot be forced
                to emit their essence.

In another dream, "I's" analyst assigned her a task: to search out buoys connected to lead weights at the bottom of the sea and pull them by going down to the bottom and swimming up with the weights, which are the shape of stars and circles. She is told in the dream that doing the task is its own reward. Work on this dream allowed "I" to form a new non-rejecting attitude toward her depressions - to release the taboo against being low, not high, stuck in the swamp, sitting in the shit - heavy and wet. "I" began to allow her depressions to serve her, to see that they carried the potential for wholeness (stars and circles) - and her ego could interact with the "leaden" affect states to do the inner work of bringing them up to consciousness for integration. The following poem arose from "I's" working with this dream:

Beloved sun-soul,
        Arise from under stone,
        Unclamp that steel
                around my heart,
        Open the gate
                to my fair home,
        Gather
                what was rent apart

Tonight, the moon
        upon my bed
Invokes
        the end of need
                to suffer lead.

DIONYSIAN AND CHRIST CONSCIOUSNESS

In a succeeding dream, "I" returns from a trip hiking in the mountains to her analyst's house where she finds herself in a below ground-level steam room, where women sit in yogi fashion alone or in groups of two and three. These images of moistening suggest a relaxing of boundaries, a movement from mind and form into emotion and flow. Water was an important element in the Eleusinian mysteries as it was for Dionysus. The effect of water working in the earth is fruitfulness — a birth. Descent and immersion conjoin. Descent replaces ascent, and wetness counteracts the dryness of too much sun. Hillman writes:

> The libido descends for refuge when driven by the excessive demands of Lycurgus, the blind tyranny of ruling will. ...Dionysus is a god of moisture, and the descent is for the sake of moistening. Depression into these depths is experienced not as defeat, but as downwardness, darkening, and becoming water.[11]

Dissolution as a theme reached its apogee in this dream:

> I encounter a young woman standing with crutches as her left foot has frozen off. ...Suddenly, she falls flat on her back hitting the wood floor with great force. She lies there stunned and in pain. Her husband doesn't seem to notice. I wait for him to pick her up. He doesn't. I go and lift her up, holding her against me with her back side against my front like a rag doll. I clasp her to me to comfort her. Suddenly, she begins to scream and writhe. Pieces of her flesh and blood

---

11 Ibid., p. 284.

seem to come out of her extremities and go splattering in all directions. I continue to hold her in horror until the flailing subsides.

An explosive breaking of all boundaries - of the most profound container, the body, splashing blood and flesh into the air. Through the horror of dissolution, "I" felt an ecstatic release from the bondage of ego domination, from instinctual repression originating almost at her origin. Hillman reminds us that Jung suggested that since dismemberment is ruled by the archetypal dominant of Dionysus, then the process, while dissolving the central control of the old king, may simultaneously be activating the pneuma distributed throughout the materializations of our complexes. Dismemberment of central control enables the resurrection of the natural light of archetypal consciousness - sparks of Dionysian spirit - held in the organs. An experience of dismemberment heralds renewal, an initiation into body consciousness through severing habitual ways one has "grown up" and "grown together".[12]

"I" remembered her mother's comment: "I did only one thing wrong with you; I made you grow up too early." The reality was that "I" was toilet-trained at ten months and started babysitting for her newborn brother when she was two years old, situations requiring extreme premature control and responsibility. No wonder the dancing, frenzied maenads, followers of Dionysus, always fascinated her. Their unfettered self-expression released inhibition to allow a great flow.

In the throes of another death-dissolution experience, "I" wrote of re-entering her body-psyche: rebirth - new life - was activated organically out of dismemberment...

---

12 Hillman, James. "Dionysus in Jung's Writings," *Facing the Gods*, Spring Publications, 1980, pp. 160-162.

"this clod, this piece of earth, that flesh is heir to"

Now, at Gary's fortieth, they dance,
   not the music of the spheres,
   but body beats, breast rhythms
   sound pulsing through arms, legs, pelvis, pores -
   a tidal wave of resonance pours through each clod:
   each enlivened unto oneself,
             unto each other -
     all to the starry Hudson river sky
     that gathers to itself
     this womb-room of revelry.

Here, in this hospital bed,
       an inert body shrouded in pain
     reaches out its every fibre to the champagne –
     Sherry said they'd toast me, my friends,
     Toast me! that like Lazarus,
         and like you,
         I may rise again.

An ever-ripening continuity, *birth* is the recurrent cosmic event that comes out of death.

Overarching "I's" whole process of grappling with animus – identification/immersion in the masculine and masochistic alienation from the feminine self was a dream she had two days before her initial interview for acceptance at the Jung Institute. The context was a state of deep brooding and self-examination about the path on which she sought to embark - that of mid-wifing psyche in the spirit of Jung - a movement out of subservience to ancient patriarchal expectations of woman's role into authentic self-syntonic service:

I was standing with a group of people on a hill which I recognized to be the hill near Gethsemane facing the city of Jerusalem. Below us was another group of people. As I looked at them, a man separated from the group and walked toward our group. I watched him coming; as he got closer, I saw he was Carl Jung, looking intently at me and carrying something in his hands. He stood before me, said brusquely, "Here's for you," and thrust into my hands a reed basket in which, to my amazement, *stood* a fish, its eye staring at me. Then he turned and walked back down the hill to his group.

Plate X

This dream led to extensive and intensive ruminations and illuminations around the symbol of the Cross and the symbol of the standing fish in the basket - a living experience of the power of a symbol to influence consciousness. Could this woman receive the full significance of the symbolic communication into consciousness for her soul's redemption? "I" has returned again and again to the image of this fish standing in the basket as a tuning instrument to awaken inner harmonics, each time reverberating to new notes. (see Plate X) The yin-yang, yoni-lingam conjunction symbolization is obvious: basket as the containing feminine principle and the erect fish as the phallic masculine principle. The fish is the enigmatic and emphatic element: animus-spirit issues predominate, it would seem. And, the standing fish does not represent the patriarchal rational sky masculine, but rather points to Dionysus and Christ and water and the irrational. "I" mulled the parable of the Loaves and Fishes, after seeing a standing fish in mosaic in the church where the wedding was to have taken place... the more one gives, the more one has... connection with the Self is a source of limitless abundance... one need not be prey to depletion, to the "not-enough" bad mother. Living into the image of the dream would mean developing an adequate, non-porous feminine-self-ego that can both contain and be sustained by creative interplay with its male counterpart, a new animus.

In the inner landscape of the dream, "I" stood in the old world of Gethsemane-Crucifixion: a suffering daughter wedded to intellectual achievement, the pristine rational values of Christian upbringing, and the non-frivolous, Puritanical work ethic, mindful always of sinful potentials. Inviting her to explore new visions of possible reality, Jung's offering to this woman on her own crucifixion cross intimated mysteries to be plumbed. Hearing the Master's gruff voice saying, "Here's for you," "I" felt a challenge - a call to "live into" and "understand" her self personally and transpersonally, to honor Jung's transmission through her life and work. Jung himself wrote about his "preoccupation with Christ, who himself is the fish (*ichthys*)" of the Fisherman Father - the Self. He goes on to say that his task was the "cure of souls" and that a dream he had of a fish laboratory and hanging pavilions for spirits reminded him that he "had not yet dealt with the major concern of "philosophical" alchemy, the *coniunctio*, and thus had not answered the question which the Christian soul put to me."[13] "I's" *task* would, it seemed, involve grappling with Christian soul-suffering, discerning along the way afflictions in the *imitatio Christi* and not forgetting the foundation-feminine element symbolized by the reed basket, harkening to the Grail cup and potential healing union through the *coincidencia oppositorum*.[14]

After this dream, "I" began to feel uneasy in churches, sitting under the spell of a bleeding Christ strung up on a huge crucifix. The image of the fish standing, its eye fixed upon her - alert - alive - related - would rise before her to blot out the agonized Christ. "I" began to seek in nature compensatory crosses, ones that vibrated life: by the sea in Maine, in the canyons of New Mexico, by a lake in Colorado, she found wooden crosses that moved and danced. She called these resurrection-earth crosses as opposed to crucifixion-heaven crosses (see page 33 also). These crosses carried the spirit of the dance of life, forming a link to the living Christ spirit "that never never dies" ...During that time she heard the folk song, "Lord of the Dance" on a tape titled "Simple Gifts" by Benjamin Luxon and Bill Crofut:

---

13 Jung, C.G. *Memories, Dreams, Reflections*, Random House, N.Y., 1989, pp. 214-215.

14 In AION, Volume 9, ii, of *The Collected Works*, Jung deals extensively with the psychology and mythology of Christianity.

I danced in the morning when the world was begun,
And I danced in the moon and the stars and the sun and
I came down from heaven and I danced on the earth
At Bethlehem I had my birth.

Chorus: Dance, then, wherever you may be,
I am the Lord of the Dance, said he
And I'll lead you all, wherever you may be,
And I'll lead you all in the dance said he.

I danced for the scribe and the pharisee,
But they would not dance and they wouldn't follow me,
I danced for the fishermen, for James and John,
They came with me and the Dance went on.

Chorus

I danced on the Sabbath and I cured the lame,
The holy people said it was a shame
They whipped and they stripped and they hung me high
And they left me there on a cross to die.

Chorus

I danced on a Friday when the sky turned black
It's hard to dance with the devil on your back.
They buried my body and they thought I'd gone,
But I am the Dance and I still go on.

Chorus

They cut me down and I lept up high,
I am the life that'll never never die.
I'll live in you if you'll live in Me,
I am the Lord of the Dance, said He.

Her attachment to the Crucified Christ was waning. The
Living Christ had found her. "I" began to feel how draining of
vital energy the actual form of the Crucifixion Cross was. In
addition, she discovered its antecedent - the equal-sided cross
of life - in New Mexico, where the Native Americans perpetu-

ate its influence. Not succumbing to the sacrificial ethos of the Calvary Cross of Christian oppressors, Native Americans use this "equi-limbed cross of Nature"[15] ceremonially and in their artistic expressions (Plate XXIV).

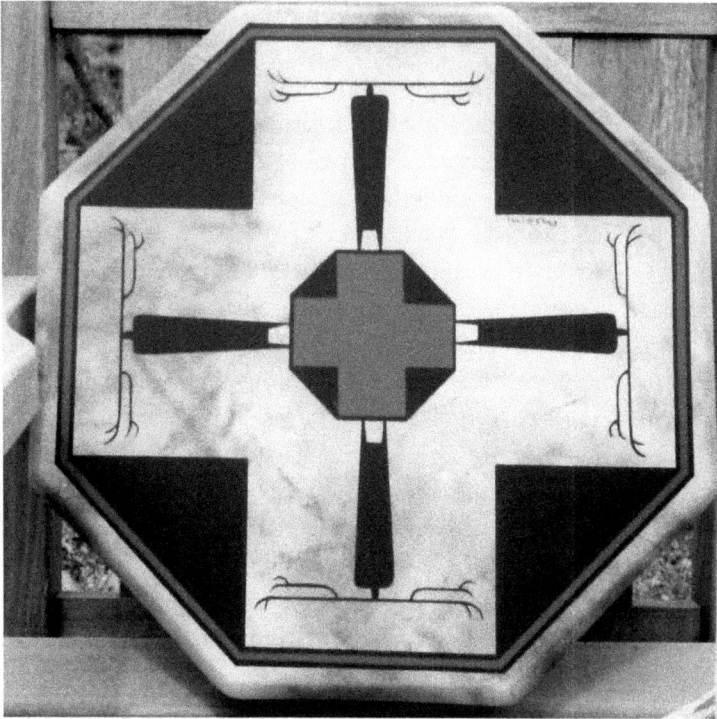

Plate XXIV

"I" encountered Matthew Fox and his book ORIGINAL BLESSING, wherein he differentiates Crucifixion Spirituality, which he calls Fall-Redemption Spirituality, from Cre-

---

15 Fortune, Dion. *Psychic Self Defense*, The Aquarian Publishing Co., London, 1930, p.183.

ation-Centered Spiritualities. The call to control passions and to see passion as a curse is opposed to Ecstasy, Eros and the celebration of passion as a blessing: climbing Jacob's Ladder is replaced by "Dancing Sara's circle". Fox became an ally for "I" in gutting out the death image indoctrination, oriented around the belief that if you are alive, you are sinful, and if you are dead, you are holy.

"I" became increasingly aware of the fact that the masochistic woman's derailment from fruitful self-development was deeply linked to the pervasive symbol of the Christian Cross. What resonance was embodied and generated by this symbol, she continued to ask? What archetypal energy was communicated and aroused within her as she contemplated the Cross? Dis-ease... Imbalance... This cross, used to punish by killing in Jesus' time and before, represented a profound distortion: the horizontal axis was raised from a central position on the vertical axis to correspond to outstretched human arms from which the weight of the body hung in death - no welcoming open arms represented here! This symbol, linked to death and incorporating an elevated and truncated horizontal-earth-axis, displaces the feminine-earth-body element upward toward the head, heaven and spirit. The raised horizontal axis signifies the feminine lifted off the ground - idealized, rather than real and earthy, made into an object and available for exploitation as she is disconnected from her nature. Earth is not given equal measure with Heaven. The Goddess is raped as the ascending elongated yang member thrusts upward away from earth toward the spiritual and mental, abrogating any possibility of heaven- on-earth in which the vital opposites are integrated. [See again the dream image of integrated opposites: the vessel-soul (reed basket) contains and grounds phallos-spirit (fish). (Plate X)]

"I," through contemplating her dream experience, realized how stuck she was in the Suffering-Sacrifice segment of the Mysteries of Transformation. Had Jung thrust the fish into her hands to dispel the darkness of the world of feeling (suffering and martyrdom) within which she had long been encapsulated? "I" had received from Jung the feeling sense he communicated in a letter to Hildegard Kirsch:

> "Somewhere there seems to be great kindness in the abysmal darkness of the Deity."[16]

At the time of the dream, "I" was fixated upon a Christ betrayed by Judas in the Garden of Gethsemane, sweating blood in his agony before the increased agony of his crucifixion pilgrimage. Since her birth, in fact, "I" had trod the dismal path, her inner world lit by the black sun of depression, isolation, and separation from her self, while outwardly she was a bright performer. The world of feeling represented by her mother and father, both alienated from the Goddess and the earth, was so negative that she had cut herself off from her heart, turning feeling to stone and finding refuge in the bastion of the mind.

How to depotentiate this old consciousness wedded to suffering and create a new consciousness that embraces suffering as a prerequisite for joy? How to move from the sterile wasteland of Osiris betrayed and scattered piecemeal through the land of the psyche to a restored totality such as is represented by Isis and her sister Nepthys collecting the bones of the dead Osiris to "re-member" him? How to move to a feeling, not just thinking, experience related to the ecstatic recognition of rebirth and renewed creativity - Horus BORN from Isis and Osiris, Christ BORN of Mary and the Divine Spirit! "I" could start to remember the truth she had long forgotten: that suffering the death of the old order precedes the *joy* and *celebration* of the resurrection. She recognized that there is death but also

---

16   Kirsch, Hildegard. "Reveries on Jung," *Professional Reports 2* (March 1975): 1-14.

there is no death, only rebirth and ongoing evolution: the dance of death *is* the dance of life.

Scrutiny of the Christian cross reveals that in one sense it has no center as it cannot be contained in the Circle, rendering it impotent as a communicator of union and wholeness. On the other hand, the original archetypal Cross with its equal arms is a powerful ancient symbol expressing an active reconciliation of the conflicting opposites. This Cross implies a circle and its members intersect in the center of the circle, a point signifying Spirit Manifest, a geometric gateway for incarnation, which symbolizes "the process of ongoing creating"[17] through the incarnation of spirit into matter, divine into human, etc. In the balanced cross, division is healed and duality resolved, bringing peace to the Cosmos. Mandalas of Tibetan Buddhism depict the quadrated circle as cosmic axis. (see Plates I, V)

Plate I

---

17   Howell, Alice O. *Jungian Symbolism in Astrology*, The Theosophical Publishing House, Wheaton, IL, 1987, p. 75.

Plate V

J.W. Perry has researched in depth the symbolism of the quadrated circle. He found that the simplest form of the quadrated circle is the SUN WHEEL, containing a cross whose four arms have traditionally represented the four cardinal points, as in the Asiatic mandala the four directions or four continents. The mandala may be derived historically from the Han mirror, which is essentially a circle and cross with the sun at its center.[18] (see Figures 1-6) The Mound Builder culture in the ancient

18   Perry, J.W. *The Self in Psychotic Process*, Spring Publications. Dallas, TX, 1987, p. 92.

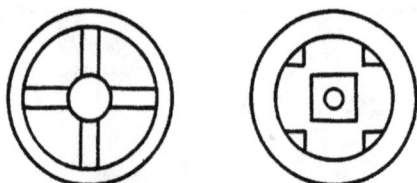

Figure 1. *a*. Diagram of sun wheel. *b*. Diagram of Han mirro

Figure 2. Emblem of
Akkadian sun-god.

Figure 3. Emblem of
Akkadian sky-god.

Figure 4. Sun wheels. *a*. Mycenaean. *b*. Greek.

Figure 5. Sun wheels, *a*. Swiss lake dwellers. *b*. Gallic.

Figure 6. Sun wheels. *a*. Dakotas. *b*. Mississippi.

Figure 1-6

pre-colonization America of the Mississippi Valley also had as a major symbol a balanced sun-disc cross (see Plate II). A contemporary rendition of the balanced cross (see Plate III) relates to the earth and the four elements through the animal carvings on each of the four arms (cougar-fire, hummingbird-air, snake-earth, dolphin-water). At the center is a rose, symbolizing what T.S. Eliot implied when he wrote at the end of the *Four Quartets* "the rose and the fire are one" - what "I" experiences as the incarnational point in the center of the cross-circle.

Plate II

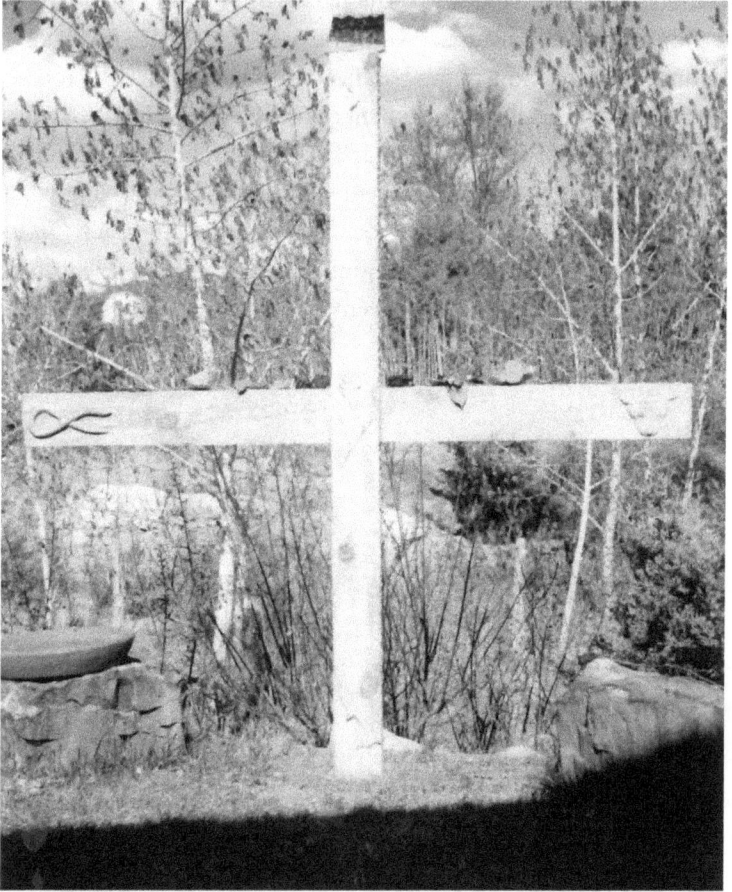

Plate III

Thomas Inman, discussing the cross as derived from the sun wheel, makes a special point of the solar and lunar signs in the figures, indicating the concept of the mystery of the sexual conjunction of male and female powers as a fertility principle. Perry provides the following information about the dynamic forces infusing the symbol of the balanced [Christian] cross:

...Similarly, Drews argues that the Christian cross was related to the crossed sticks used in the ancient Vedic rites, namely, the cult of Agni, the fire god. These fire-boring ceremonies were designed, by sympathetic magic, to renew the sun at dawn. A flame was ignited by the friction of sticks in a boring motion, a single male one being twirled where it penetrated the exact center of the cross formed by the two female ones, the arani. Typical nativity symbolism pertained throughout the rite, of especial interest here since it represents the Divine Child brought forth at the center of the maternal cross. The particularly impressive ceremony was held at dawn on the day of the winter solstice, the time most myths of that part of the world assigned to the birth of the god. "As soon as the spark shown in the 'maternal bosom,' the soft underpart of the wood, it was treated as an 'infant child.'" The GHRITA, the juice of the cow, and the SOMA, the juice of the plant, were poured over the fire, now raised on the altar; "from this time 'Agni' was called 'the anointed.'" Gods (kings) and herdsmen hastened to pay reverence;" the new-born Agni already had become 'the teacher' of all living creatures, 'the wisest of the wise.'" The end of the time of darkness and the beginning of the holy season were celebrated, and "Agni and the other Gods again returned to men, and the priests announced to the people the 'joyful tidings' ...that the Light God had been born again."[19]

"I" felt the radiation of the root symbol through this "old-new" cross she had not seen in the churches of her time. She envisioned the ceremonies aimed to renew the sun daily at dawn and yearly at the winter solstice. She felt in the cross the force of fire, the kindling of the divine spark. Fire - the sun ...love - is the generative element and from its transformations all things

19 Ibid., p.95.

are born: "Condensed fire becomes steam, becomes earth."
(Heraclitus) Jung found in the symbolism of fire-boring "a key
to tracing the liberation of libido for cultural creativity through
the work of the symbol."[20]

"I" was surprised to learn that Christ was not generally
shown crucified on the Cross until the Middle Ages: in the 11th
century the dead or dying Savior shown on the Cross revealed
that he was seen as the sacrificial victim (the Paschal Lamb) -
the intensification within the Catholic church of Christ's martyr
role to which women resonated. "I" compensated for her deflat-
ed sense of self by allying herself, thus inflating her value, with
the Suffering Christ. Attached to her suffering and companioned
by the Crucified Christ, she wrote the following poem:

O Crucified Christ
      What, my lover, art thou now?
You, a man, strung up upon the tree,
Mirror for me my martyrdom.
One - of all your kind -
You died for me, I was told -
As I have died for You through aeons old.
Sundered from my self
      in mistrust of brutal male,
You restore my faith in man so bold.

You take the spear into YOUR heart,
      the nails into YOUR palms, not mine.
You and I - one entity -
      Man and woman -
         sans mercie.

---

20   Ibid., p. 87.

Here was an image of male to whom she could connect. They could dance the victim's dance together, die together, if unable to love and live together.

In unearthing information around the slow unfolding of the symbolism of the Cross in Christianity, "I" discovered that originally Jesus' head was placed before the Cross in the orb of the sun or his whole body in the center of the Cross in the center of the circle, thus representing Christ as sun, i.e., the divine man — a representative of the Source of all Life, *not* a Dying Ember. Perry writes, "He was not only at the center of the cross... but equivalent to the cross."[21] And, according to Didron, "the cross is more than a figure of Christ; it is in iconography Christ himself or his symbol."[22] The medieval figure of the enthroned Christ was represented in the midst of a circle with the four evangelists, or their theriomorphic representative, at the cardinal points; this is analogous to the Egyptian designs of the four sons of the sun-god Horus standing on the lotus.[23]

"I" realized one day, in contemplating the equal-sided cross, that its vitality also emanates from the relationship of the central cross point to the human body chakra configuration: the intersection point of the beams of the cross is analogous to the area of the human body at the base of the spine of the first chakra, the root-survival chakra. The root chakra (the grounding-earth area in the human energy field) corresponds to the center of the circle, where the transcendent incarnates into human form. Since the Christian Crucifixion Cross has no center and cannot be contained in a circle, that symbol has been rendered impotent. It denies the source of Divinity and

---

21 Ibid., p. 87.

22 Discussions of the symbol's evolution are in: Hastings, *Encyclopedia of Religion and Ethics*, Vol. IV, pp. 322-399.

23 Jung C. G. *Psychologie and Alchemie*, p. 286, Abb. 101, 102.

distorts the sacred content of the Cross into a symbol of suffer-ing. In the Mayan teachings, "I" discovered, chakra one at the horizontal beam of the balanced cross was designated as K'UL, the "sacred-God-vibration". The coccyx was known to be the sacred place where solar energy is deposited at the base of the spine to be utilized for conscious awakening and evolution.[24]

Jung's offering to "I" of a live fish erect in a basket, its eye focused upon her, was so jarring, so incongruous, that she was thrown off balance. Her focus on Christ's agony shifted as her attention was drawn into the eye of the fish toward a new consciousness. What energy does this upright, vertical, aware fish-form generate? What is the significance for "I" of this *co-niunctio symbol*? And he had said, "this is for you." Was it a guiding image suggesting the possibility of holy union between her feminine self and the creative masculine within? She re-membered that somewhere Jung had written, "The union of opposites on a higher level of consciousness is not a rational thing, nor is it a matter of will; it is a process of psychic devel-opment that expresses itself in symbols."[25]

"I's" descent from her stone cross of years of joyless strug-gle and emotional numbness was expressed in a dream:

> I'm hanging onto a red granite column-cross that is in water. I'm above the water, holding on to the top. It starts to swing back and forth and then moves onto an island, entering a grand house; the entrance hall is painted cornflower blue so vivid that I exclaim with joy. The walls are of carved hon-ey-colored wood, so incredibly beautiful. The cross moves

---

24 Hunbatz Men. *Secrets of Mayan Science/Religion*, Bear & Company, Santa Fe, NM, 1990, pp. 128-135.

25 Jung C.G., *Alchemical Studies*, The Collected Works of C.G. Jung, Vol. 13, Princeton, page 307.

with me hanging on. I come to a big mirror, I see my guide
- I'm on the ground now – I look up and see the face of a
Greek-god type young man with little curls - he comes toward
me and we kiss.

In this dream it appears that, through reflection, the petrification of the patriarchal animus is resolved and humanized
through Eros-relatedness, opening up "I's" capacity to embrace
her feeling and intuition. An animus-identified martyr woman
descends from her cross to make a conscious relationship to her
feeling life. Prior to these changes, she rarely felt her feelings: as
a response to harsh treatment from her mother who would say,
"You are so hard," and other adults, like a Christian Sunday
School teacher who said in front of the class, ""I's" soul is as
black as her hair," "I" had hardened her heart against experiences of joyful life-affirming eroticism. Her subjective world
began to be passionately fired after this descent from the rigid
world of mental forms permeated with cold self-judgments - a
masochistically self-annihilating patriarchal landscape where
she had lived, but where the goddess cannot. "I" joins her voice
with a modern theologian's "Litany of Deliverance," helping to
redeem the wounds of woman, the earth, and man himself; for
whoever wounds another, wounds him/her self as well:

From Patriarchy's dualism,
From Patriarchy's proneness to self-pity,
From Patriarchy's sentimentalism,
From Patriarchy's violence,
From Patriarchy's lack of imagination,
From Patriarchy's intellectual laziness,
From Patriarchy's lack of authentic curiosity,
From Patriarchy's separation of head and body,
From Patriarchy's separation of body from feelings,

From Patriarchy's preoccupation with sex,
From Patriarchy's fear of intimacy
From Patriarchy's cosmic loneliness,
From Patriarchy's crucifixion of Mother Earth,
From Patriarchy's forgetfulness of beauty and art,
From Patriarchy's impotence to heal,
From Patriarchy's sado-masochism,
From Patriarchy's lack of balance,
From Patriarchy's quest for immortality,
From Patriarchy's ego,
From Patriarchy's human chauvinism,
From Patriarchy's matricide,
                    Spare us, O Divine One. [26]

The Eros-animus, like the young man in "I's" dream, brings with him the creative fire, awakening the spirit and imagination to develop the seed of psyche. "I" developed a new enthusiasm and a compassionate relationship to her self after this profound encounter.

The fixity of "I's" martyr position clearly was dissolving; by clinging to the animus-cross, she had avoided getting wet and putting her feet on the ground, hence splitting from the unconscious and her own ego-self. That the cross began to move and transported her to an eros contact suggests another facet in the symbolism of the cross. "I" began to imagine *moving* crosses - crosses that were not rigid and static, crosses that moved and flowed (see Plates IV, VI, VII) and which synchronistically presented themselves to her in the outer world. She felt enlivened. She remembered the cross in the circle related to the sun wheel... the sun that continually circles the earth like

---

26   Fox, Matthew. *The Coming of the Cosmic Christ*, Harper & Row, San Francisco, 1988, pp. 250-251.

Plate IV

Plate VI

Plate VII

a great wheel... crosses that dance - the Nataraja Hindu symbol of the great cosmic dance within a circle (see Plate VIII).
The intersecting limbs (see Plate IX) began to rotate. All life is
movement, change, development, growth... Nature's process is
movement, the end of movement is death. "I" resonated with
these new images of Resurrection - Dancing Crosses. These
symbols generated an inner sense of aliveness, the renewal of a
passion for her self - she felt spring and summer after years of
winter.

Plate VIII

Plate IX

As in his Resurrection, Christ rose like a phoenix out of the ashes of his death, so "I" struggled to leap internally out of the death grip of her father's critical cynicism, out of her mistrust of her own vision and authority, out of her self-sacrificial denigration and other-orientation into a radical self-embrace: she dared to hug her own soul, to hear her own music and to dance her own dance, as Christ did in "Lord of the Dance." She remembered the psychiatrist Carl Hammerschlag's telling of his own personal healing interaction with a very ill old Pueblo priest and clan chief whom he was treating in the hospital:

Suddenly, there was this beautiful smile, and he asked me, "Where did you learn to heal?"

Although I assumed my academic credentials would mean little to the old man, I responded almost by rote, rattling off my medical education, internship and certification.

Again the beatific smile and another question: "Do you know how to dance?"

...I answered that, sure, I like to dance; and I shuffled a little at his bedside. Santiago chuckled, got out of bed, and, short of breath, began to show me his dance.

"You must be able to dance if you are to heal people," he said.

"And will you teach me your steps?" I asked, indulging the aging priest.

Santiago nodded. "Yes, I can teach you my steps, but you will have to hear your own music." [27]

For "I" the old paradigm of suffering and selfless sacrifice as an offering *to oneself* and to the world, promulgated by the Church and the image of the Crucifixion Cross, has been superceded by a new paradigm of the Great Self*ishness* (a thrust to love and nourish her self in order to love and nourish others) with its accompanying image, the Dancing Cross of Resurrected Love. The so-called new paradigm actually unveils a hidden truth, for the idea of resurrection was meant to be the center and mainspring of Christian thought. Edouard Schure writes about resurrection:

> To interpret it, to understand it, to bring it into line with the laws of the universe, is necessary, but merely to suppress it robs Christianity of its light and strength. In losing the immortality of the soul, it would lose its chief lever.[28]

---

27 Hammerschlag, Carl. *The Dancing Healers*, Harper & Row, San Francisco, 1988, pp. 9-10.

28 Schure, Edouard. *From Sphinx to Christ*, Harper & Row, San Francisco, 1970.

The Resurrection can be considered a feminine mystery celebrating "eternal process" in the soul incarnating again and again on earth and discarnating again and again. To dance the dance of one's true self is to dance in synchrony with the Self - the Cosmos. One is in harmony with the Music of the Spheres: it is said that at the autumnal Mysteries honoring Demeter, goddess of earth and corn, at Eleusis on the Greek seacoast, "they provided a natural epiphany that was apparently so striking it *elicited not sadness* from the participants but *exalted wonder*."[29] On the last night of initiation, a torch dance was performed by the pilgrims. According to Euripedes, at that point in the Eleusinian ceremonies:

> the starry heaven of Zeus begins to dance, also the moon and the daughters of Nereus, the goddesses of the sea and the overflowing rivers — all dance in honor of the golden -crowned maiden and her holy mother.[30]

It seems the torch bearing pilgrims may have followed choreographics mirroring those of the stars... advanced the science of the Cosmos, of turning cycles, changing but continuous forms, and returning measures. The author refers to the Greek writer Lucian who said,

> Dancing came into being at the beginning of all things, with Eros the ancient one, for we see this primeval dancing set forth in the choral dance of the constellations, and in the planets and fixed stars, their interweaving and interchange and orderly harmony."[31]

29 Munro, Eleanor. *On Glory Roads*, Thames & Hudson, NY, 1987, p. 136. (my emphasis)
30 Euripedes, *ION*, lines 1078-86.
31 Munro. Op.Cit., p. 138.

The metaphor of the cosmic dance, profoundly expressed in the image of the dancing god, Shiva (Plate VIII), reveals the understanding that all life is part of a great rhythmic process of creation and destruction, of death and rebirth. Shiva's dance symbolizes this eternal coming of life from death which goes on in endless cycles. Christianity repressed this experience and understanding in sundering the life-death-life rhythm. Instead, hanging on the cross of death "for dear life' has allowed the germ of creative life, the Divine Child, to languish in the human psyche. "I" came to realize she could choose 'the right death' to make way for renewed life. She could die to the death-in-life of old prohibitions, defenses, and self-negation.

The ancient Mayas and Mexicas of South America also realized in their rituals and through their symbols that cyclical laws unite human beings and nature is eternal movement with its measure (the Absolute Being was called Giver of Movement and Measure). Xochipilli, the adored Goddess of the Mexicas, represented the Milky Way, where energy is in perpetual movement, giving life and bodily and spiritual energy to all living beings. In honor of Xochipilli, "whose Visage is impassive, but her heart overflows with joy," the people sang, made Poetry, and danced.[32]

The writer of OF GLORY ROADS recounts how Christ, some time between his entry into Jerusalem and the night at Gethsemane, took his twelve friends into a courtyard and stood them around him like a circle of stones, holding hands and answering "Amen" to each line he sang, while all of them danced the star-dance of dances, singing,

I will be born/and I will bear...
I will be saved/and I will save...

---

32 Hunbatz Men. Op. Cit, p. 40.

I will pipe/ dance, all of you...
To the universe/belongs the dancer...[33]

To dance implies resurrection - ongoing life - merging one-self with nature. The dance is a metaphor for transcendence of death - NOT to crucify one's nature with its passions and desires, but to connect consciously to the "I AM" personally and transpersonally.

In the Dance, the split off Pan-Dionysus aspect of the Christ archetype is reclaimed: the Christian concept of human nature polarized into "lower" (i.e., body, woman, earth, senses) and "higher" (spirit, male, heaven, mind) is reintegrated. The New Troubadours from Findhorn on a tape titled "Love Is" sing a song connecting Jesus to his pagan roots:

On Christmas morning, so they say,
Pan sat down his pipes to play,
Restored the fairies, sprites and elves,
On woodland fields of streams and dells,
He played his pipes and the sap ran high,
While rivers coursed down the mountainside...
The deer and the joy and the flowers swayed,
Nature danced while the great Pan played.

But on this morning, so they say,
A new God came, his flutes to play,
Jesus by name, he was young and fair,
With golden sunlight for his hair.
He sat with Pan on the side of the hill,
And as he spoke, all the world was still.
You ask who I am, my brother Pan,
I am the Song of the birth of man.

33 Munro. Op. Cit, p. 141.

He raised his flute and he played his song;
It was as if the world had gone,
In its place was a blazing light,
A new star flaming in the depths of night,
And from that Light came a mighty sound,
The song of life freed from all its bounds...
The song of the One by whom the earth was made,
All this was there when Jesus played.

Hey, hey, Jesus, your song is good,
Its tune goes well with my rocks and woods,
It moves my heart and fulfills my dreams,
So spoke the god of the fields and streams.
Then both these gods, one young, one old,
They picked up their pipes and they played twofold...
They played as one that Christmas morn,
And that is how our new world was born.

"I," in wondering about the standing fish in her dream, pondered Christ's Dionysian shadow. Christ is presented by the Church as castrated from his pagan roots, cut off from his Dionysian-Eros phallic mother-earth side. The fish, as a denizen of the sea, has always been associated with the maternal waters of life - the sea womb out of which all life was birthed as the ego emerges out of the unconscious. Dionysus was sometimes portrayed with a fish at his side - the standing fish is erect, a symbol embodying the synthesis of the creative phallic masculine principle and the feminine Eros-love principle. (Eros was, after all, the son of Aphrodite, the goddess of love born from her father's severed genitals thrown upon the sea.)

Resurrecting in her psyche the phallus of Christ requires an extraction for "I" of her Mary Magdalene shadow from the Mary-mother's idealized ego-identification - for sexuality and her body to be claimed as clean. Envisioning Christ's eros-connection to Mary Magdalene enabled "I" to love her erotic earth being and, at the same time, to embrace a healed image of Christ-Jesus as both spiritual and sensual.

Returning to the vision of the standing fish, its eye searing itself into her 'suffering' soul, "I" found it was time to claim Dionysus more intensively — to reconnect to her secret hero of college days when the rational mind held sway and Apollo was all the rage. Dionysus, she remembered, was the great joy lover, who expressed not contempt and disregard for materiality, but a celebration for all of nature.

The religious tradition represented by Dionysus does not hold to the fixed and separate realities of matter and spirit, with the physical world and that of the spirit inexorably opposed — a conflict resolved only by vanquishing the world of matter. Dionysus is called "the god of wine, the god of abandon, the great liberator, the god of ecstasy. He represents the continual rebirth of life in the spring, the irrational wisdom of the senses, and the soul's transcendence."[34]

Irrational knowledge is gained through the senses, not through our rational thought processes. The way of Dionysus is to receive the world instinctively on a sensuous, intuitive level rather than in an abstract, logical, distanced way. Dionysian ecstasy is found in the sensuous world, the world of poets and artists and dreamers, who reflect the life of the spirit as seen through the senses. Connecting to Dionysian energy, "I" awakened to a heightened awareness of joy repressed. Part of the story of this half-mortal, half-god personification of divine ecstasy captivated "I's" imagination with intimations of a reality replete with sacred profanity (*the literal meaning of profanity is "outside the temple"*). Ecstatic experience debased by patri-

---

34 Johnson, Robert. *Ecstasy*, Harper & Row, San Francisco, 1987, p.11.

archal Christian attitudes could be retrieved from the underworld. "I" liked the description of the travels of Dionysus:

> The raving Dionysus left his home on Mt. Nysa and began to
> travel the world . He was accompanied by a startling array
> of followers: his tutor, the fat drunkard Silenus, rode precar-
> iously on a donkey; grinning satyrs, joyous nymphs, pranc-
> ing centaurs, and other woodland spirits capered and danced
> alongside. For human followers he had the Maenads. These
> bold women of the mountains, initiates of the ancient wom-
> en's mysteries, worshipped their god with singing, dancing,
> and bloody feasts. Together, they cut a swath of wild and
> joyous celebration across the ancient world.
>
> In time, Rhea (earth mother) purified the young god of
> his madness and initiated him into her mysteries, the very
> secret women's mysteries. The power of Dionysus was then
> unparalleled.
>
> Wherever Dionysus went he invited people to join in his
> celebration. One thing soon became clear: those who chose to
> worship him experienced divine ecstasy; those who opposed
> chose madness.[35]

Offered as spiritual nourishment primarily images of the
victimized, crucified Christ, "I" realized that she had been
starving for life -- she was creatively malnourished. Dionysus
became a portal to her feminine self - *her* body and blood, *her*
spontaneous assertive, "wild," fierce force. To connect to the
Dionysian way, "the dancing universe: the ceaseless flow of
energy going through an infinite variety of patterns"[36], is to
restore in and through her individual self the life-embracing

35 Ibid., p. 78.
36 Capra, Fritzjof. *The Tao of Physics*, Shambala, Boston, 1991, p. 244.

element to the figure of Christ. It is to transmute suffering into joy, the pain of life and the body into the sensuous/erotic tradition that appreciates beauty and the arts: consider the Dionysian character of the Minoan culture, for example. Reintegrating the ecstatic element into the Christian Transformation Mysteries releases the Crucifixion Fixation, no longer denying the Resurrection-Rebirth process of union of the divine with the earthly, of life and love that never dies.

Jesus as Christ - the manifestation on earth of heaven in the heart - can be made whole in our psyches through restoring to consciousness his split-off dynamic Dionysian shadow. In fact, Jesus' inherent connection to the Greek-pagan Dionysus is pointed to in metaphoric statements like the one in John 15:1 ff. when Jesus says, "I am the *vine*; you are the branches." Robert Johnson also points out that the Christian Antioch chalice shows Christ swinging on a seat of grapevines, poised between two worlds, "a clear reference to the Dionysian precedent"[37] that indicates ecstatic religious experience:

Joy, divine spark of the Gods,
daughter of Elysium
we enter your sanctuary drunk with fire.
Your magic reunites
what custom has sternly parted.
All men become brothers
where your gentle wings rest.

"Ode to Joy" by Schiller

Through its emphasis on the Crucifixion, Christianity symbolically made Christ the God of one season only — winter,

---

37   Johnson, R. Op. Cit., p. 31.

when the frost kills the green life of the earth. He is remembered only as sorrowing and suffering. Dionysus, like Christ, knew heart-rending grief, but he was remembered with Demeter (Earth Mother-corn Goddess) at the harvest time celebration of the Eleusinian Mysteries, which centered on an experience of reaping, of fruition, of rebirth. Worshippers were shown "an ear of corn which had been reaped in silence".[38] Edith Hamilton writes of the connection between these two great deities, who represent Divine creative play on earth:

> Beside Demeter when the cymbals sound
> Enthroned sits Dionysus of the flowing hair.
> It was natural that they should be worshipped together,
> both divinities of the good gifts of earth, both present in the
> homely daily acts that life depends on, the breaking of bread
> and the drinking of the wine. The harvest was Dionysus' festival, too, when the grapes were brought to the winepress.[39]

In the Catholic Church, however, these festival seasons are called "Ordinary Time," with almost no celebration. Far into the unconscious has been relegated the quiet, potent vegetative element - the pure star that shines amid the gathering of the fruit.

"I" felt great compassion for Christ-in-her, in-everyone, strapped on the wheel of suffering turning inexorably - denied for centuries the dance of resurrecting life - a grief and immobility waiting for release in her own "dance."

In the Church of the Loaves and Fishes in Nazareth, "I" found herself staring with wonder at a mosaic depiction of a vertical fish - intimations of Jesus' split-off phallic creativity

---

38   Hamilton, Edith. *Mythology*, Penguin, Inc., NY, 1969, p. 48
39   Ibid., p. 49.

and generativity. She reflected on the dismembering of Osiris by Set, his dark brother, activated by the will-to-power, and suddenly saw and felt how the Church Fathers had dismembered Jesus, the Divine Man. It was Isis and her sister Nepthys who searched the world, found, and re-membered Osiris. These women revivified-resurrected the broken male force. Again she saw and felt the ancient ceremony of the raising of the *djed* - a giant tree trunk prone on the earth, the dead depotentiated phallus gradually being uplifted until it stood fully erect, head in the sky and base of the ground, linking earth and spirit. "I", too, searches to find within herself the phallus of Jesus - the creative potency of love. "I" seeks to abandon her lifelong identification with the Virgin Mary, pure in perfection, who hovers off the ground and devotes herself to service to others, exclusive rather than inclusive of her own needs and desires.

The Dionysian spirit continued to insinuate itself into "I's" psyche through dreams. She worked in Jungian analysis to amplify her personality by consciously relating to this energy repressed in childhood. Possession of her psyche by the patriarchal spirit, abetted by an identification with the judgmental and suffering Christ, was so entrenched that it was resistant to change; long ago these old deities had staked their claim to her psyche. Now the work of subjective transformation was her own.

An early encounter with the Dionysian spirit trying to live itself in her occurred in the following dream:

I'm at a workshop at a center for religious and psychological studies. A large room has been cleared for two young women (17 years old, maybe) to entertain. The first, who looks like a young me, starts a dance — she is flowing gracefully to the music, "modern" dance style, when all of a sudden she speeds up, gets all out of sync and falls slightly (I realize she's trying to do everything all at once and it's too much). An older woman (one known to the dreamer as "animus-possessed" — i.e., always "right," unswervingly one- pointed in perceptions, dominant in any situation) looks at the music director and says, "Don't let her be/fall in love." I take exception, saying, "Love for the music is good; it will allow her to be in the flow with herself and the music and not become all harassed and disjointed by having to perform." The girl comes back to center stage and stands still while the music plays in order to attune herself. I know she'll be alright now.

"I's" ego gets in the way of trusting herself as a carrier of creativity, not allowing the fruits to do the speaking. She wards off her erotic Dionysian energy, repressing the phallic sexuality and energy of the Goddess. She realized she was walking a tightrope, supported on one side by the instinct to love (eros-relatedness linking her self to her Self) and threatened on the other side by her old other-oriented "performance," avoidance way of being. It was safe for "I" to stay a statue, avoiding the fear of her dance not being received. A personality such as hers in the thrall of the Christian ethos must struggle painfully to experience willful, conscious engagement with repressed passion. Guilt quenches exuberance as the "sin" of bodily pleasure which, as "I" can now see, camouflages the presumed "sin" of spiritual ecstasy - the so-called forbidden fruit of the individual inner journey to the numinous within — or what Jung called "the recognition of a greater personality (that) seems to burst an iron ring round the heart."[40]
Another dream pushed "I" further toward the hidden promise:

---

40 Jung, C.G. "Concerning Rebirth", *The Archetypes and the Collective Unconscious*, Vol. 9. 1, Princeton University Press, 1977, p. 122.

I am in a turtle enclosure at a nature center in the water playing with the large turtles. I rub the backs of two as they swim
past. Suddenly, nearby in the shallow water, a turtle stands
up on its back legs to reveal a beautifully designed belly and
does a dance, smiling. I am overjoyed and awed by this turtle's happy vitality and self-revelation. (see Plate XI)

Plate XI

The next morning a T-shirt arrived in the mail from a Native American friend: screen-printed on the front was a dancing
turtle! "I" felt the urgency "to get out of her shell" - to start to
do her dance of self-manifestation and self-expression - to *show*
her self, to take her light out from under a bushel basket, as a
close friend put it. This turtle (in *The Medicine Cards* denoted
as a symbol of Grounding and Mother Earth - a call to honor
the Creative within and "to observe my situation with motherly compassion"[41]) invited "I" to dance, not just on earth, but

---

41   Sams, Jamie and Carson, David. *Medicine Cards: The Discovery of
Power Through the Ways of Animals*, Bear & Co., Santa Fe, NM, 1988, p.77.

in the water - to feel her physical vitality, to feel her emotions, to ground her soul in the unconscious matrix. "Turtle" urges one to use water and earth energies - to flow with situations, to move organically between inner and outer - to flow slow, to move in a grounded way. (Remember — "Daily she walks behind the cows.")

"I's" resistance to incorporating Dionysian energy into her 'Christian' identity was underscored in the following experiences she wrote about:

> Chased by Christ am I
>> As "He" seeks to heal himself in me;
>> "He" waits while I establish
>> my daughter at college;
>> "He" follows to the home
>> in the mountains
> where aging parents dwell;
>> On the full moon
>> of 8/28/88,
>> I awaken from a dream:

In the dream, I had boldly written these two terse sentences upon a large blank sheet of brown paper posted on the *living* room wall of a little old house a woman friend (someone in the process of dismantling an old lifestyle focused on superficial materialistic values in order to claim a simpler, more inward way) has just bought and is redecorating:

> DIONYSUS HAS OFFERED HIMSELF TO YOU.
> WELCOME HIM!

My friend comes in looking shocked. I apologize, saying I *spontaneously* felt I *had to* write these words from a dream on the paper. She's fascinated I've let loose and exposed my dream; she asks me what I think the message is. I shout, "I don't have to be consistent anymore! I can free myself!"

She then reveals that people have been asking her how come she hangs out with me, as I'm strange and incomprehensible. (end of dream)

Such an injunction! WELCOME DIONYSUS! When the god comes, he MUST be obeyed, he MUST be given hospitality. Not to embrace Dionysus is to invite madness, to be cursed, the stories tell. "I" could continue to close the door on Dionysus only at great peril to her "individuation" journey. Dionysus demanded a reversal of the patterns of her old dance wherein she served the masculine and men! Now she MUST receive male energy as a guide to her own depths — to trust he is no longer user and oppressor but grace-giving inseminator. All will be changed; Thoreau was right when he said, "Consistency is the hobgoblin of little minds." "I" will no longer be predictable, but "strange," inbued by Dionysus, "The Loosener" of control, as she leaves the Saturn-father force field to enter the realm of the living Self.

"I" wrote a poem after she had this dream, as she struggled for new self-consciousness:

> I rode the mare of pain,
>   I rode her through the rain,
>   through the valley of death,
>   Yea, I feared the evil
>   feared to straddle her fully
>   in the ride
>   where no guide did lead...
> Devoted was I to the throes
>   of death without life
>   crucifixion *sans* resurrection
>   the passion of pain,

Dionysus slain.
Despair reigned
        in psyche's kingdom of the shoreless sea
        where a drowned child
                struggles to be reborn
                in a white swan's wings.

And then on the Seventh Day, a dream day,
        the Turtle Danced
        the Fish Stood Up
                in his reed basket
                and Stared at me —
                Jung said gruffly, "Here's for you."
        memory inscribed on the room's bare wall,
        "Dionysus has offered himself to you,
        Welcome him!"

Lame woman,
        paralyzed with fear,
        ruts carved in old earth,
Where are your ears?
Where are your eyes?
Where is your tongue?
Where is your birth?
What more can the gods do for you?

How dare you refuse
this grand invitation
        to the dance of dismemberment?

Dare I stall, after all,
while peaches reduce to embers?
Such a ploy
        to introduce joy
                to a cripple!

Again and again "He" had tried to break through the strictures of pure intellectual mind and order to awaken "I" so that she might claim her own knowing through felt-experience - her own intuitive wisdom; to embrace her muse - to write poetry; and, to "speak" - to manifest herself in the outer world, to stop swallowing her sound as she usually did at moments of trial. Not to welcome Dionysus as "a bridging animus-figure" who fleshes her Persephone nature into "a woman who gives birth" would be to close the portals to what Bachofen called "the source both of her sensual and transcendent hopes."[42] Opening the door to Dionysus, she is now able to experience eros within, to relate to herself.

Ten years before, Jung had presented her with the standing fish in the basket. Now an unambiguous, non-symbolic injunction to complete the Dionysian initiation experience, similar in essence to 'psychological fertility' rites participated in by Roman women who also longed for a sense of wholeness.

In the Roman initiation ceremonies depicted on a series of ten murals, an object believed to be the divine is contained in a mystic basket; part of the rite involves an uncovering of the phallus of Dionysus, symbolizing a primal regenerative force. In an underworld encounter with the Dionysian spirit, an initiate would experience "the magnetism of animal power."[43] Jung in his "Vision Seminars" stated that one scene with a faun and goats and Silenus exemplifies a woman's becoming aware, through a loosening of conscious control, of her absolute connection with nature. Bradway writes that at the end of the initiation,

---

42   Bachofen, Johann. *Myth, Religions and Mother Right*, N.Y., Bollingen Foundation, 1967.

43   Bradway, Katherine. *Villa of Mysteries: Pompeii Initiation Rites of Women*, C.G. Jung Institute of San Francisco, 1982, p. 25.

The initiate is dancing the dance of the arisen spirit. She has no need of music outside herself; she makes her own music with the clashing of her cymbals. The scarf, the representation or the symbol of the feminine, is flowing out around her, and the staff, or thyrsus such as Dionysus carries, is being held for her by the priestess who is acting as her attendant. It is as though the feminine and masculine are available for her as she needs them. She has fully experienced the power of each, but she is in the power of neither. She is one-in-herself. She is free.[44]

The day of her "Dionysus" dream, driving many miles across North Carolina, "I" had listened again and again to the song, "Lord of the Dance." She felt the life spirit that won't be diminished: the Dionysus-Christ affirmation of the possibilities of Heaven-on-Earth. She felt joyful, no longer cynical and depressed. She knew clearly that nothing ever dies, for rebirth and resurrection and reincarnation are embedded in the very nature of things. "I" felt the imperative to dance her own cosmic dance - to seek to live in testimony to a non-demonic way, that of honoring her daemon, creative spirit as it entered her being.

For a Catholic Christian girl trained to remain contained, whose spacious spirit was domesticated in infancy, welcoming the essence of Dionysus into the multiple levels of her being (physically, emotionally, mentally and spiritually) was a radical response - a revolutionary act. Old scruples and reticence flung to the winds, she became receptive to her instinctive, chaotic, teeming depths.

Her "wild" soul freed, "I" could finally choose to move 2,000 miles from north-east to south-west, an aesthetically satisfying, self-consonant landscape that helped to evoke her

---

44   Ibid., p. 27.

sensuality: a place replete with emptiness in its vast vistas of sky; redolent of beauty in painted cliffs, green mountains, crystal streams; resonant with silence within which the living word is *felt* and *heard*; where the dance is still danced, for the earth-keepers (Native Americans) are there.

D.H. Lawrence wrote the following of his experience in New Mexico:

> I had no permanent feeling of religion till I came to New Mexico and penetrated into the old human race-experience there... a sense of living religion from the Red Indians... never shall I forget watching the dancers, the men with the fox-skin swaying down from their bottocks, file out at San Geronimo, and the women with seed rattles following... Never shall I forget the utter absorption of the dance, so quiet, so steadily, timelessly rhythmic and silent, with the ceaseless downtread, always to the earth center, ... Never shall I forget the deep singing of the men at the drum, swelling and sinking, ... deeper than thunder ... the deep sound of men calling to the unspeakable depths.[45]

To potentiate Dionysus as an "archetypal image of inde-structible life"[46] as he was in Greek religion, considered pagan by the Christian religion, is to redeem the spirit of resurrection, for "indestructible" means without death as a finality. With the image of Christ-Crucified (destructible-life) no longer predominating, psyche will cease to be motivated by a potent anti-life energy. To reunite in one's self the Dionysian arche-

45 Hillerman, Tony, ed. *The Spell Of New Mexico*, Lawrence, D.H., "New Mexico," University of New Mexico Press, Albuquerque, 1976, pp. 32-34.

46 Kerenyi, C. *Dionysus*, Bollingen Series, LXV, 2, Princeton University Press, Princeton, 1976.

typal image with the Christian archetype makes one available for what Goethe perceived as possible when he wrote, "Perhaps in this way we shall attain the high philosophical goal of perceiving how the divine life in man is joined in all innocence with animal life."[47] The concept of sin is implicitly transcended here: in reclaiming innocence, the schism between the sensual and spiritual is simultaneously healed. To return theriomorphic attributes (dolphin, standing fish, cow, lioness, for example) to the god-goddess image in the psyche of the unconscious imitator of the suffering Christ ("I") means that the "Christ who liveth in me" becomes the carrier of the whole spectrum of life energies from the animal-instinctual realm to the transpersonal. God-Goddess is no longer truncated, split off from His-Her animal shadow. "I" realized that animals symbolize different aspects of human consciousness. They are symbolic of certain spiritual and transcendental truths, carrying within themselves the union of spirit *and* instinct.

On the first evening at her new house, "I" stood on the flat roof offering gratitude for the Great Spirit's blessings. Her back was to the sunset facing north. Racing toward her came a black speck, like a tiny sky torpedo on a direct mark; it dive-bombed the top of her head, just grazing her with its wings and sped away to the south. Afterwards, she wrote the following poem:

---

47 Ibid., quoted from frontspiece.

Ode to a Hummingbird

O hummingbird, presence evanescent,
life's nectar you seek and find –
I have pined for you
      these many years,
You have come with greetings,
      a swift torpedo
      plummeting from the sunset sky
      in answer to my heart's call.

Did you come
      to dub me joyful,
      to welcome a traveller home at last,
      the end of long years' fast,
      of roots longing for rightful earth?

Did you come
      to cast out fear,
      to pour your spirit into pain's receptacle,
      reminding a doubt-filled soul
      that joy is respectable?

O hummingbird,
Companion on the Path,
      fortitude in flight,
      Inspire motion
            to dart my solitary way
            across vast inner skies
            to reach the radiant Heart
            where Love is fired...

THE GODDESS

Throughout her search for Her Self, "I" surrounded herself with images, manifestations of feminine empowerment,
with which she interacted internally. Botticelli's sweet light-
filled Madonnas of her past were replaced by images such
as the Black Madonna of Rocamadour (Plates XII, XIII).

Plate XII

Plate XIII

"I" encountered her in a chapel in Southern France, without prior knowledge of her history. For at least an hour, the two were alone, contemplating each other. The Virgin emanated a still yet dynamic composure, a force of conviction that is *related*, not negatively "self-centered," and streams forth from her center. One-in-herself ("virgin" in fullness of being and self-relatedness - i.e., woman with an integrated positive animus), she is available to others but not lost in them. She is the dark wisdom of the earth and nature - wisdom gleaned from having suffered herself, not the naive Virgin with her son Jesus as role models who suffer only *for* others, not themselves. The Black Madonna image helps to rehabilitate in the unconscious the martyr-image of "virtuous" suffering ("unselfish" since it is not supposed to benefit the sufferer). It helps to recover the true mythologem of the transformation mysteries, which the original Christ myth was connected to: the mythologem of a soul that moves from unconsciously suffering its fate to consciously suffering itself in terms of learning to carry one's own cross meaningfully, as Jesus and Mary actually did. Jung wrote that individuation is the endeavor to make what fate intends to do with us entirely our own intention. Suffering *for* others aborts the process of one's own soul-making. What is more, suffering *for* others is a violation of them, for they are then denied the opportunity to learn what their suffering aims to teach.

Later, in Egypt, "I" encountered the Black Sekhmet, the daughter of the sun god Ra, alone in her own small temple within the great temple complex of Karnak on the Nile. (see Plate XIV) There she stood, gleaming black granite, lion-headed, firmly benign, but not to be trafficked with, surely. Her vision penetrates the dark unconscious with the luminous light of the sun which, as "I" stood peering at her with flashlight in hand, suddenly projected itself through an aperture in the roof to illuminate her staff and forehead, symbols of her phallic strength, will-power, and the assertion of her knowing. She stood revealed, black and gold — the union of the opposites of dark and light, death and life, matter and spirit, stone and sun.

Plate XIV

In beholding Sekhmet holding the staff and with the sun's emphasis on the staff, "I" was shown an image she could appreciate — a feminine being who has incorporated the masculine into herself. Instead of being overwhelmed by and subsumed "under" the yang force, masculine energy is accessible to serve her and for her to serve with it. Having assimilated her feminine nature as well, she has the power to stand alone, for she is whole. It is important to note here that in Egypt the powerful integrated feminine - the woman who can stand alone - is usually represented as having a consort, who is also integrated and fully her equal, not inferior nor superior. Sekhmet's consort was Ptah, a creator-god of wisdom. The major sacred couple in Egyptian religion were Isis and Osiris. In Greece, Dionysus and Ariadne were a divine pair, with Dionysus as "the archetypal reality of *zoe* (life-force)" and Ariadne "the archetypal reality of the bestowal of soul, of what makes a living creature an individual."[48] *Zoe* requires soul for life conception. In the schema of creation, Dionysus *requires* Ariadne, Isis *requires* Osiris.

These archetypal images of humanized divine couples compensate for a vacuum in Christian symbolism which focuses on such unbalanced pairings as Mary the Mother and Jesus the Son. The archetype of the royal couple and coupling was banished from consciousness by the Church, and became anathema, rather than an erotic spiritual goal much to be desired. This goal has been transmitted underground in the esoteric spiritual traditions through secret stories of the Christ and Mary Magdalene, the Grail legends, statues of the Black Madonna hidden in caves to be protected from destruction by the Catholic Church, scrolls of teachings secreted in vases and buried in desert sands.

In Egypt, "I" was witness in that numinous moment to Sekhmet's function as the solar eye channelling the solar principle - her father the sun - onto Earth and her radiation of the light of consciousness into the darkness of physical nature. In Her, the Christ energy is born: matter, soul and psyche are infused with the creative light force of spirit. The instinctual and spiritual are one. Like Christ, she is both tough *and* compassionate. "I" invoked her presence in a poem:

---

48   ibid.

How can my heart
    meet the feather of Maat,
        not too light
        not too heavy
    a steady weight
    of good deeds, love and wisdom?

Sekhmet, dark lioness,
    help me play my part:
        your furrowed brow
        eyes golden glowering
        compassion, yes, but
        not consolation
            for petty kingdoms.

Plate XV

A direct meeting with a Goddess manifestation in Nature occurred for "I" during a hike in a remote river canyon
in Northern New Mexico. Huddled under the root mass of
an uprooted, long-dead, gigantic ponderosa pine, she noticed
within the tangle of thick roots what looked like breasts. As
she looked more intently, the form of a woman emerged (Plate
XV). The woman was in the throes of giving birth, her head
twisted and her mouth contorted in a scream; one arm pointed
skyward, the other towards earth, linking her to both worlds.

This root-Womb Goddess, as "I" called Her, made her synchronistic epiphany when "I" was "remembering" herself after the removal of a fibroid-ridden uterus. During that time "I" was also immersed in a book called *Women of Wisdom* by Tsultrim Allione that introduced her to the Dakini tradition of the Goddess in Tibetan Buddhism. After meeting the Root Goddess, "I" wrote a poem:

> Out of her hurt
> > healing is birthed
> Out of her wounds
> > love's blood pours forth.
> I puncture you
> > that you may give
> I pierce you
> > that compassion's flame ignite.
> your womb, no longer tomb,
> > bursts open to the light
> your heart groans
> > in joyful anguish -
> > a great cry
> > for the bright dawning
> > > of Love Incarnate.

"I" realized that nothing could be taken from her, nothing had been lost; in fact, removing her uterus had created a gateway for connection to her true womb: to the ever-present, indestructible matrix of life in her and outside of her, screaming to be consciously related to. She committed herself to live *rooted* in the earth, in her creative source-place, remembering once more that there is both death and no death, for every loss is a resurrection door of initiation into new perception and potential.

Plate XVI

The black lioness Dakini image (Plate XVI) continues to imbue "I" with feelings of dynamic creative life expression. She is centeredness-in-motion, while the Black Madonna and Karnak-Sekhmet are centeredness-in-stillness. All represent enlightened energy in the female form. The dakini-goddess is black (earth/death), gold (solar/light) haloed with red (blood/ passion/fire). Allione writes that the redness relates to "primordial lust, the passion which binds the universe together."[49] In Tibetan tradition, the red also connotes feminine menstrual blood and suggests the burning interior power of women, "primal matrix which can become babies, milk, passion, fierceness, primal lava of life."[50]

Particularly provocative for "I" is the *fierceness* of the lioness, as her own fierce nature had been muted by Virgin-Mary-perfect-passivity. Her passionate intensity, considered dangerous and duly repressed, received confirmation from the lionesses.

Invoking and visualizing this dynamic female manifestation activates the energy to blast the constrictions of old inhibiting patterns - to dance into the maelstrom of everchanging flow. A great insult to the Self is to stand still - to be static and not to evolve. The interplay of motion and stillness is a possible achievement. Maintaining balance, however, requires vigilance since these opposites tend to polarize between the inner directed and outer directed. Contemplating those feminine images provides for "I" an inner experience of the harmonious interweaving of the primal yin-yang elements.

Finally, recently, "I" found an image of the feminine that redeems emphatically in its expression the masochistically thwarted instinctual level by encompassing the full range of self-creativity from the spiritual to the bodily. (Plate XVII) This painting entitled "Hagia Sophia" by Meinrad Craighead impressed "I" as a compensatory image for, perhaps even a "take

49 Alione, Tsultrim. *Women of Wisdom*, Routledge & Kegan Paul, Boston, 1984, p. 34.
50 Ibid.

Plate XVII

off" on, the ungrounded Virgin of Guadalupe, who stands on a sliver moon in the heavens, her delicate hands touching in prayer, her downcast eyes looking modestly toward those on earth from on high. (Plate XVIII) Hagia Sophia, on the other hand, sits bare-breasted on the firmament within a corona of shamanic animal fangs with the rhythmic monthly moon cycles of growth and change represented in the four corners. Her fleshy hand holds the thread to the amazing maze of gut-intuitive wisdom. She is gross, mundane, clearly *of the earth*. She is the earth, she is BODY, em*bodi*ment *par excellance*. She is feminine, organic knowledge accessible to each incarnate soul. Experience of HER is visceral, not conceptual or abstract. She reveals the truth that everything, all experience, is written on the body. On her shoulders sit two owls — totem birds of the seer, the one who sees into darkness and other dimensions. Craighead writes in her litany to Hagia Sophia:

> "O Seat of Wisdom enthrone us, we beseech thee: Lady Wisdom threads the labyrinth of her womb and each of us begins our journey to her center, our pilgrimage to the Holy Land. Doth not Wisdom cry out? ... throughout the moons of our life span?"[51]

This Madonna with her intense gaze turned inward and outward at once compels "I" to listen internally: "Power is within, enfleshed; I am wisdom here on earth, in Nature... in your nature... I am available *now*. I am heavy and light, empty and full, here and elsewhere... I *am* at the dark of the moon and at its bright fullness... I wax and I wane... I am blind and I see... Woman, earth and spirit, am I, forever dying and forever awakening..." ("I's" own words)

In *her*, spirituality is no longer separate from nature: she is the primordial feminine with power to give birth, bearing the primal quality of fertility and potentiality. She is not just grounded, but the ground of being, for the occurrence of creation is a *birth* process: the world is born, not made.

---

51 Craighead, Meinrad. *The Litany of the Great River*, Paulist Press, NY, 1991, p. 44.

Plate XVII

As "I" experienced the incarnation in her self of the ch-
thonic shadow feminine, she became able to protect her heretofore masochistic self from incursions of the sadistic male force,
whether it came at her from outside through men or women or
from inside as aggressive self-denigration. She could say "no"
to demands to serve that were not in her best interest, hence
masochistic; she learned to ask the question, "What does this
serve?" and make conscious decisions in her interactions and
allocations of energy. She no longer felt a pawn of her parents
and the parental complexes. In fact, this attention to her self
required a long period of separation from her father and from
her mother, in order that she might organize her self around
these new imperatives.

Connection to her own phallic animus, rather than domination and victimization by it, created the ground for a new relationship to the yang solar spirit principle. "I's" psyche found
a resonant mirror in ancient Egypt's Queen Hatshepsut:

> Not a petty stone
> > stands in Karnak
> Every pebble
> > reeks with significance.

> Hatshepsut's obelisks
> > pierce the sky,
> > penetrate to the quick
> > > of Amon-Ra.

> How mighty is
> > her stiletto thrust
> > of still stone
> > into the power
> > > that imbued her!

"I's" nascent relationship to indwelling power enabled a
return to the creative potency of the Higher Self.

THE DOLPHIN

In her continuing circumambulation of the symbol-image of the standing fish in the reed basket, "I" fell into a reverie: suddenly she found herself in the sea with dolphins - sublime creatures who for years had hovered on the periphery of her consciousness. Implied in the symbol of the standing fish *is* the dolphin, she realized. The fish in actuality is a horizontal creature. It is cold-blooded, devoid of an "emotional body," far removed from human consciousness and displaying behavior patterns vastly different from the dolphin species, who are mammals *and* conscious. It is no accident that Dionysus was portrayed as accompanied by dolphins on the famous cup from Vulci, now in Munich, painted by Exekias. (Plate XIX) Dionysus and dolphin have an integral connection as expressions of *zoe*.

Plate XIX

Dolphins are known to be extraordinarily intelligent and aware. They have their own highly developed language (the average dolphin has 10,000 words at its command and speaks in syllables) and communication skills, and even relate telepathically to humans. The research of Dr. John Lilly, who has studied dolphin intelligence for over a decade, has revealed that the dolphin brain is not just "almost equal to ours" but "every bit our equal" or "vastly superior." Emotionally, dolphins express a range of feelings from joy to depression, including empathy and humor.

By writers such as Aristotle and Aesop, Heroditus and the Plinys, dolphins were presented as suffering from no such aggressive feelings as the Greek gods who were continually at war. Rather, dolphins were viewed as helpful, generous, and understanding. The significance of the dolphin to the Greeks can be felt in the following two translations of a poem by the Greek historian Oppian of Cilicia (200 AD.):

So Dolphins teem, whom subject Fish revere
And show the smiling Seas their infant-Heir
All other Kinds, whom Parent-Seas confine,
Dolphins excell, that Race is all Divine,
Dolphins were men (Tradition holds the Tale)
Laborious swains bred on the Tuscan Vale;
Transformed by Bacchus, and by Neptune loved,
They all the pleasures of the deep improved.
When new-made fish the God's command obeyed,
Plunged in the Waves and untried Fins displayed,
No further charge relenting Bacchus wrought,
Nor have the dolphins all the men forgot;
The conscious Soul remains her former thought.

* * *

Diviner than the dolphin
is nothing yet created;
for indeed they were
aforetime men and lived
in cities along with mortals...
They exchanged the land
                for the sea
            and put in the form of fishes;
but even now the righteous spirit
        of men in them
preserves human thought
        and human deeds.[52]

The image here is of two kinds of human beings: land-humans and water-humans. Oppian suggests an "original" connection between humans and dolphins. The Greek word for dolphin is *delphys* and comes from the word *delphis*, meaning womb. The dolphin is thus pictured as the living womb in the sea of creation. According to the great priest/historian Berossus, the Chaldean, the Maya descended to earth in the form of a fish (dolphin, I think), bringing their culture. For the Dogon of Mali (a remote African tribe) as well, their creation myth centers around Nommo (see Figure 7), the collective name for the great culture hero and founder of civilization who came from the Sirius system in the form of a dolphin to establish societies here on Earth.[53]

In Sumeria, considered by many to be the birthplace of our civilization, one finds the founding Savior figure of Oannes - a half man, half fish-dolphin, who brought all the civilizing arts

---

52   Stewart, David. "Our Father Who Art in Water", *Simply Living*, No. 11,12, Shree Media Publications PTY LTD., Australia,1980, pp.24-37, 60-70.
53   ibid.

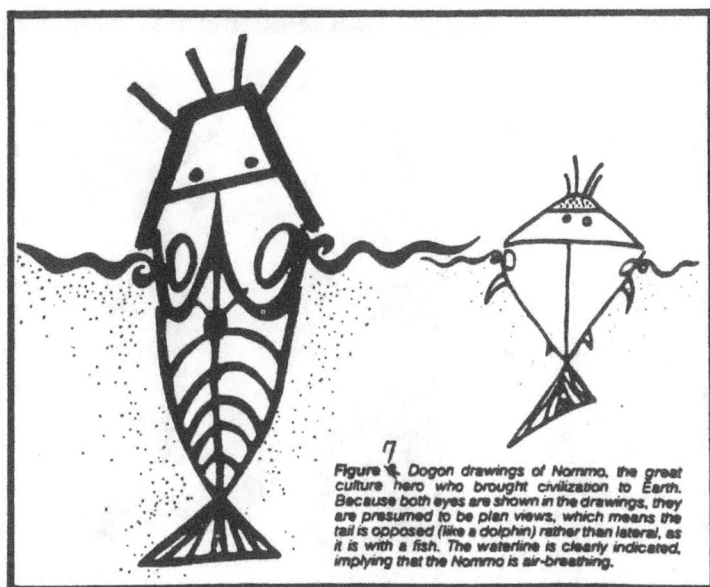

Figure 7. Dogon drawings of Nommo, the great culture hero who brought civilization to Earth. Because both eyes are shown in the drawings, they are presumed to be plan views, which means the tail is opposed (like a dolphin) rather than lateral, as it is with a fish. The waterline is clearly indicated, implying that the Nommo is air-breathing.

Figure 7

Plate XX

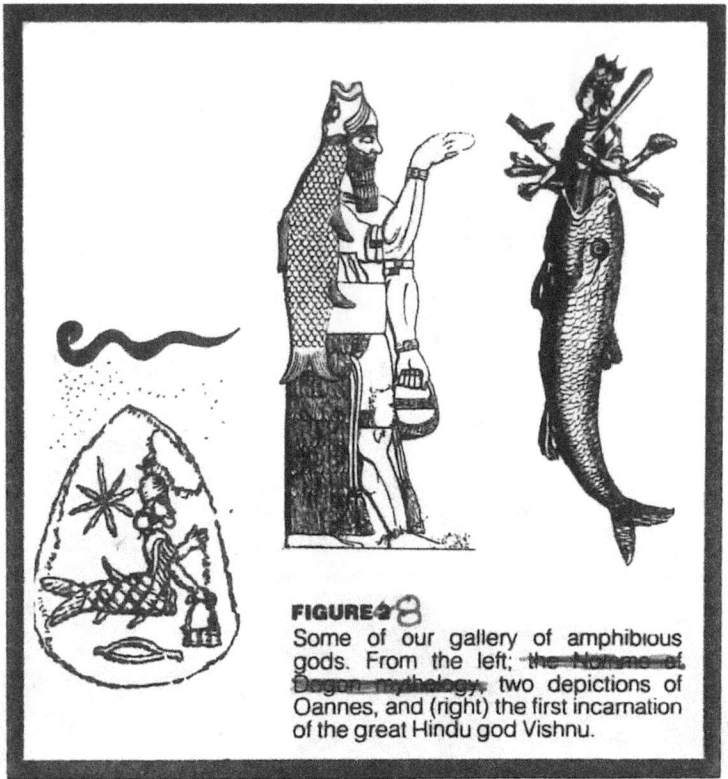

FIGURE 8
Some of our gallery of amphibious gods. From the left; the Nommo of Dogon mythology, two depictions of Oannes, and (right) the first incarnation of the great Hindu god Vishnu.

Figure 8

to Sumeria. (see Figure 8) When one looks to the beginnings of Indian culture, we see the Hindu Redeemer god Vishnu, another teacher of the civilizing arts, in his first incarnation as part dolphin, part human: the dolphin is the womb-container which supports him and out of which he emerges. (Plate XX) The Nabateans, an Arabian people who built a flourishing culture in a remote desert region 500 years before Christ, worshipped the dolphin in the form of Attargatis, who was the lunar goddess of the waters and of love and fecundity. Her son, Ichthys, was the Sacred Fish, who, they believed, was their creator and sustainer through life. The fish as the symbol of the life germ represents the realization that all life has its origin in water.

The standing fish (dolphin-womb) for "I" has come to represent spirit in matter evolving and moving toward the transcendent Self - i.e., rebirth (born again into the divine) and renewal as a rite of passage, a reemergence from the water-womb place of origin into the light of consciousness. What is expressed is the passage of the soul from matter to spirit or the movement from unconsciousness, the watery depths, to spiritual understanding. The fish-dolphin symbolism relates to the age-old ceremony of baptism: the original meaning of baptism, as celebrated in Babylon, was a re-enactment of man's survival after the great deluge and was thus a celebration to Oannes, the Babylonian fish-god.

Christianity assimilated the "pagan" baptism "survival" celebration of Oannes: the Christians retained the important place of the dolphin in the ceremony of baptism. In Matthew 4:19 Jesus says: "I will make you fishers of men," suggesting the spiritual awakening that baptism will effect. The emblem of the dolphin appears on baptismal fonts, on gravestones, and on Christian coffin lids, emphasizing that birth (*womb-delphys*) is the essential element in death. Manly Hall writes that the dolphin was accepted by the early Christians as an emblem of Christ, because the pagans had viewed this creature as a friend and benefactor of humankind. He adds that the heir to the throne of France, the *Dauphin*, may have secured his title from "this ancient pagan symbol of the divine preservative power."[54]

"I," out of her dolphin ruminations, has been increasingly drawn to dolphin-energy as reflecting an original way of "human-being" long lost. It is on the back of the Dolphin that Eros

---

54   Cory, Issac Preston. *Ancient Fragments*, London, 1832, quoted in Hall, Manly P., *The Secret Teachings Of All Ages*, the Philosophical Research Society, Inc., Los Angeles, 1977, p. LXXXV.

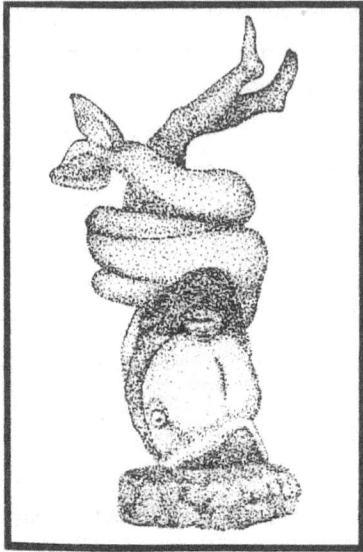

Figure 9

Plate XXI

PlateXXII

rides: the Dolphin is the vehicle, the communicator, for Eros-Love Relatedness. (see Figure 9 and Plates XXI, XXII)

With both solar and lunar associations, Dolphin carries in its being a potent image of wholeness. Connected with Apollo Delphinos, it is light and the sun, but also the feminine principle on account of the aforementioned connection between *delphis* [dolphin] and *delphys* [womb]. The dolphin, in fact, appears quite androgynous: the male genitals retract into a womb-pouch when not in use. Dolphins seem to be living representatives of yin-yang balance - models of a human-related life form in harmony with itself and with each other.

Dolphins are known to attend lovingly and compassionately to each other. Jim Nollman tells of a species of dolphin documented as holding its own funeral service.[55] Thomas Merton wrote, "Compassion is the keen awareness of the interdepen-

---

55   Nollman, Jim. *Dolphin Dreamtime*, Bantam, N.Y., 1987, p. 64.

dence of all living things which are all part of one another and involved in one another."[56] And incidentally, the Hebrew verb RHM, usually translated as "to have mercy or compassion" derives from a root that means "womb," another to dolphin as carrier of the primal life-giving related feminine element.

"I" entertains the notion that it is allowable, if not imperative, that she consciously "suffer" ("womb" - feel motherly, love or mercy for) herself, not in the old sense but in the sense of what Jesus did during his Passion at Gethsemane. Suffering herself has come to mean befriending her own passions, her deepest feelings of ecstasy and pain, love and alienation. The author of Proverbs elaborates the same idea: "If a person is mean to herself, to whom will she be good?"[57]

"I" is coming to understand that suffering *for* others as she was told Christ did for her was self-abnegation, not compassion. True compassion consists in *assisting* her self *and* others to carry the crosses of conscious incarnation, of having been made flesh ("carne," "meat").

True compassion *unites* us in a common field. Kabir, the great fifteenth century mystic of India, celebrates this kind of connectedness:

I am like a pitcher of clay floating in the water, water inside, water outside. Now suddenly with a touch of the guru the pitcher is broken. Inside, outside, O friends, all one.[58]

---

56 Merton, T., address delivered during the conference on East-West monastic dialogue (10 December 1968), quoted in Religious Education, Vol. 73 (1978), p. 292.

57 Proverbs 14:5,6.

58 Kuman, Sehdev. *The Vision of Kabir*, (Concord, Ontario, Canada: Alpha & Omega), 1984, p. 183.

The dualism of inside and outside is broken through. Divine and human are no longer separated. "As above... so below," say the alchemists.

To paraphrase Wordsworth, "How like a dolphin came "I" down," for she has since childhood wanted to serve and to heal others. Dolphins are not polarized between service to self and service to others. In relinquishing her masochistic posture of self-denial and self-wounding, "I" found that relationship was not an "either... or" but a "both... and." Dolphins historically have been known to be saviors of the wounded at sea. The idea of service without self-sacrifice is an organic part of their compassionate natures, not a debatable issue. The basic nature of dolphin, it appears, is love incarnate, a capacity to love themselves and others that has not been distorted or truncated. They manifest an axiom that has been stated as *"souls love to love."*[59] Plutarch wrote,

"To the dolphin alone, beyond all others, nature has granted what the best philosophers seek: friendship for no advantage. Though it has no need at all of any man, yet it is a genial friend to all and has helped many."[60]

Jesus Christ, the teacher, incarnated love for its own sake as the healing elixir. "I" never forgot John Yungblut's telling in a lecture of the apostle Peter, who was someone not even a mother could love, but Jesus' unconditional love of Peter's essential being transformed Peter's negative sense of self and consequently his "unlovable" behavior. Dolphins are known to

59   Brooke Medicine Eagle. *Buffalo Woman Comes Singing*, Ballantine Books, NY, 1991, p. 225.

60   Cherniss, H., and Helmbold, W.C. (trans. ed.) Plutarch, *De Sollertia Animalium* 36. Cambridge, MA., Harvard University Press, 1957.

relate to autistic children in a Christ-like way, guiding them out of their remote withdrawn states into self-expression.

Dolphin energy has literally been on the planet from earliest recorded history. It is the other original sentient consciousness on the planet, an evolved heart-mind-body-spirit energy, from the likes of which the human species has progressively devolved. Cetaceans (dolphins and whales) have remained in earth's oceans and in the sea of the collective unconscious as a translation of the idea of healing service and love into physical form, providing a reminder of humanity's potential.

"I" coming full circle in her pilgrimage to her self-Self, can now solidify the integration of classical pagan roots into her Christian soul. She can consciously live into the revelation that "a True Christian is a Pagan" and help others raise their Pagan-Christian inner children, such as the wild, golden-eyed girl child, who recently made her appearance in a woman's dream with the dream mother saying she is not a decent Christian child fit to be cared for. The dance with the Dolphin Christ is ongoing - so "I" is learning to laugh... The God-self celebrated now is not the aloof, controlled and controlling patriarch of heaven, but rather the Creator God of earth and water, who enters dynamically into creation and *urges one to eat of the apple.* Meister Eckhart, a Christian mystic, says that this God, who is "voluptuous and delicious" and the Maker of all that is voluptuous and delicious, dances and becomes tickled with joy. Andre Lorde, the black feminist poet, writes:

> A feminine spirituality as distinct from a patriarchal one will value the erotic and teach us disciplines of erotic celebrating, creating, and justice-making... an assertion of the life force of women.[61]

---

61 Lederer, Laura, ed. *Take Back the Night: Women on Pornography*; Lorde, Andre, "Uses of the Erotic: the Erotic as Power," NY, 1980, pp. 297-300.

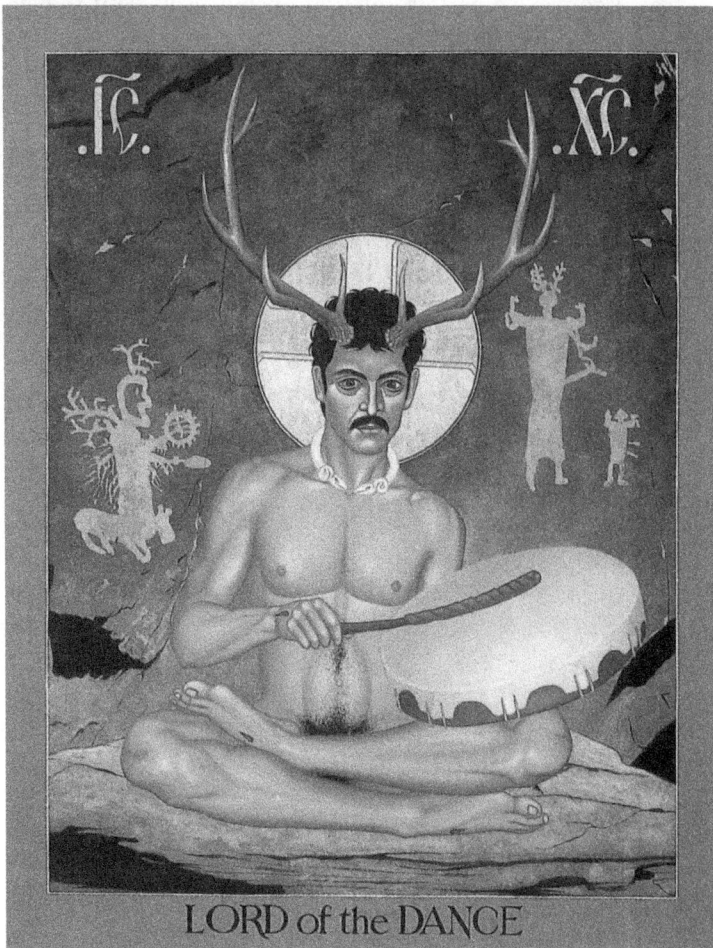

LORD of the DANCE

Plate XXIII

A contemporary Catholic icon painter, trying to imbue the Christ Archetype with new energy, recently produced his rendition of the Lord of the Dance. This image integrates the old Celtic horned god, the Christ, and the Native American deer medicine, as well as male and female. (Plate XXIII) This portrayal conveys a certain integration but leaves out the element of joyful creativity. Perhaps he is *about* to dance - on the threshold, readying himself for the return to consciousness of a great influx of creative potency.

When the suffering-addicted woman descends from her cross and sheds her masochism, she wills to take on the "stigma" of self-orientation and exultation of the spirit. To resurrect means to be reborn, i.e., to embrace Eros — the link of love to one's own being and to all consciousness in all life forms on earth and in the cosmos. The affect associated with resurrection, Dionysian ecstasy, is the ability to stand outside ego boundaries and experience the flow of life within and without. Linking an individual to loving understanding, which is the crux of therapeutics (healing processes), can be accompanied by joy. Working on oneself analytically, for instance, need not be just a process of suffering oneself in the sense of undergoing a *painful process* of change. Originally, "to suffer" meant also to undergo or experience any process, not just negative. What about revelling in oneself, loving- understanding oneself? Where is the affect of affirmation? Too one-sidedly "I" had been devoted to living psychologically in a space labelled "negative inflation" - the hubris of deeming herself "the most wounded," "the most agonized," "the most crucified, victimized, desecrated" of souls.

This negative inflation has been fostered not just by crucifixion symbolism, but by another Christian mytholgem, namely the dyad of mother and son, whose interpersonal roles are to suffer *for* each other, not creative union of male and female, husband and wife. The transformative-creative Egyptian trinity of Isis-Osiris-Horus, for instance, wherein the *coniunctio* of male and female leads to an expression of spirit in flesh (the Divine Child), has been minimized in the Father-Son-Holy Ghost trinity within which there is no *coniunctio* imagery of male-female union producing wholeness. The Christian image stresses, rather, male-union, father unity with son abetted by an ethereal, sexless "ghost" presence. The Christian soul must look to alchemy or Egypt for paradigms of psychological soul evolution, where the archetype of the *coniunctio* represented by the sacred triangle is alive as a reality in the collective unconscious.

The mother-son dyad, the primary couple in Christianity, denies the primacy of male-female union, fixates on the maternal role of the feminine, and elevates the element of self-sacrifice. Mary, we are led to believe, lives a life totally devoted to her son. Her *raison d'etre* is to be for him - first as womb, then as nurturer and supporter through his trials. She is presented as the consummate good mother-womb. It is inconceivable that she would make any demands for herself. She is totally assimilated to her martyrdom: a GOOD PERFECT Woman, just as Georgiana was and "I" originally was.

Robert Johnson confirms "I's" understanding when he writes that we have looked only at Jesus' suffering and taken it to ourselves in order to feel that we are "good" and that we have forgotten such messages as one coming from a Hindu saint who said, "The best way possible to worship God is simply to be happy."[62] Joseph Campbell exhorted the masses to "Follow your bliss," not your pain, to pursue what provides *joy*. Clearly, the *way* does not have to be a way of unmitigated pain split off from the opposite polarity of play. Evelyn Eaton, a woman who steeped herself in the Native American Way, wrote a paean to delight:

Wankun Tanka [Great Spirit] is the Deity of JOY. Of joy and lightness, and of song and dance. And of everything that is beautiful and is lovely and heart-lifting.

---

62 Johnson. Op Cit., p. 31.

Tears are good, but laughter is even a more important
remedy. ... We seem to be growing through suffering, growing through sorrow. That's *our* fault.

...So the Grandfathers only care about our growing ...
if we won't grow in the sunshine, they send the rain and the
hail... so it's our own fault if we insist on growing through
suffering. We should grow through joy.[63]

The experience of happiness has been rendered frivolous
and vapid, a mark of unconsciousness, by the belief that only
suffering is the roadway to consciousness. Enduring trials and
tribulations to compensate for one's sinful nature is inculcated
as the highest good.

63   Eaton, Terry. *Joy Before Night*, The Theosophical Publishing House,
Wheaton, IL, 1988, pp. 149-150.

IV

Finale

"I" stands on a point in time awaiting rebirth on earth, a healing of her spiritual- psychological disorientation. "I" seeks to reclaim a self-integrity lost since the first Eden, with the apotheosis of the will-to-power and the Western European emphasis on death as a finality, not an act of transition into the other life. The Egyptians, the Mayans, all the esoteric Mysteries carry the secret knowledge that, like Nut the great Sky goddess who swallowed the sun at night to birth it each morning, we die in the night to be born again the next day. The great wheel does not stop turning. "I" continues to embrace consciously the spirit of Resurrection, of Dionysus, of the Dolphin, of the great Goddess. The Christ is no longer fractured into the old man-Saturn (depicted in Byzantine mosaics as the Christ-Pantocrator) and the mother's dying son. The True Christ, reanimated in the soul, seeks to enable a human embodiment of love-in-action as a thread in the web of a new Incarnation, transforming the *love of power into the power of love* through the holy marriage of soul and spirit, psyche and eros. "I" can dream of moving toward wholeness as the *lumen naturae* finds its way into her soul's dark night.

HYMN TO OSIRIS

The doors of perception open; what was hidden has been revealed. It is myself I see and a thousand colors of swirling liquid light. I am where the sun sets below the mountains. I am in this body. I am the star rising above clouds hung by a thread from its ocean moon. Hail myself traversing eternity walking among gods, a shuttle flying across the loom through the threads of time. This is all one place, one cloth: a man's life endures. On earth flowers grow, snakes crawl and wisdom lies in the palm of a hand. All that is will be - hawks and sparrows, the thousand lives within.

I have come home. I have entered humanhood, bound to rocks and plants, men and women, rivers and sky. I shall be with you in this and other worlds. When two greet each other in the street, I am there speaking to you. When you look up, know I am there - sun and moon pouring my love around you. All these things I am, portents, images signs. Though apart, I am a part of you. One of the million things of the universe, I am the universe too. Whatever I am, woman, cat or lotus, the same god breathes in every body. You and I together are a single creation. Neither death nor spite nor fear nor ignorance stops my love for you.

May we come and go in and out of heaven through the gates of starlight. As the houses of earth fill with dancing and song, so filled are the houses of heaven. I come, in truth. I sail a long river and row back again. It is joy to breathe under the stars. I am the sojourner destined to walk a thousand years until I arrive at myself.[1]

---

1   Elis, Normandi, trans. *Awakening Osiris: a New Translation of the Egyptian Book of the Dead*, Phanes Press, MI, 1988.

"I's" process has been leading her to her core nature, to the original ancestral Dolphin-Christ body-soul configuration and thus to the sphere of *conscious reunion* - a recovery of her heart's inclination to live in kinship with all realms. The circle continues to circulate, the tail of the uroboric serpent reaching for its mouth. T.S. Eliot acknowledged this "tale" when he wrote:

> We shall not cease from exploration
> And the end of all our exploring
> Will be to arrive where we started
> And know the place for the first time.[2]

When the great Synchronicity, the yin-yang of the opposites represented by the Dionysus-Christ—Dolphin—Dance and the Balanced Cross, comes to reside in individual human Nature and human Consciousness, Psyche — earth itself — will know Redemption.

2   Eliot, T.S. "Little Gidding," *Four Quartets,* Faber & Faber, London. 1955, p.43.

April 15, 1992

GOOD FRIDAY: Aftermath

You did not die
        for *my* sins
I will not die
        for yours...
You did not implore
        that I take your cross...

        Abhorrent lie
        Travesty of truth

In ruthless savagery
        of dismembered Love
Healer, you carried your cross
        so that I could re-member
        to carry mine,
        to wrestle my fears
        of standing
                on shifting sand
        to risk the abyss
                of Samson shorn
        and kneel before the knowledge
                that You were born...

My Hero -
          ruthless for truth
          You chose
              to throw yourself
              on the pyre of resurrection

          No ire
          No grief

You are the thief
          who steals love in the night
          to throw it, in a great comet trail,
                    to "me" -
          who calls this Friday Good.

Waves of timeless love
          transmute
        the death of my inheritance.

GOOD FRIDAY MOON

Full moon
        in blue sky

You are not shy
        to unveil in day
        your Body
          of light.

Afterword

"The cross has also the meaning of a boundary-stone between heaven and hell, since it is set up in the centre of the cosmos"[1]

C.G. Jung

"..the sun comes to shine in psyche's dark depths"

Descent From the Cross

The healing processes of transformation described in this work continued throughout Elaine's life. In later years, she encountered a book that both validated and deepened her understanding of these processes. It was J. Daniel Gunther's *Initiation in the Aeon of the Child*, which expounds on the Mysteries of *Thelema*, the spiritual philosophy that fuses the Mystery traditions of East and West, whose central edict is "Do what thou wilt shall be the whole of the Law." "Love is the law, love under will."

One of the great revelations of Thelema is that the *imago dei*, or image of god, is no longer that of Osiris – the dying rising god-man – Jesus, Attis, Adonis, Dionysus – as it was in the previous Aeon of the Father[2]. Nor is it Isis, the undifferentiated ouroboros of nature, of the earlier Aeon of the Moth-

---

1   Jung, *"Psychology and Religion: West and East"* (Collected Works Vol. 11, Princeton), page 80.

2   See Jung, *The Archetypes and The Collective Unconscious, and Aion: Researches into the Phenomenology of the Self* (Collected Works of C. G. Jung Vol. 9 Parts 1 & 2, Princeton).

er[3]. The imago dei of the current Aeon of the Child is Horus:
The radiant Solar offspring of the Mother and the Father, the
unique synthesis of both. "The new Aeon is the worship of the
spiritual made one with the material, of Horus, of the Child, of
the Future."[4] which "… has for its purpose the complete emancipation of the human race…"[5] Our image of god, and our
understanding of the Sun now is not the dying and rising sun of
the Aeon of the Father, seemingly disappearing each evening,
throwing the world into catastrophic darkness – but the eternal
Sun, ever radiant – the source of all light, life, love, and liberty,
that dieth not.

Elaine was delighted by the cosmic *conjunctio* she discovered in Thelema and in the nature of Horus – the sacred synthesis of male and female, and the fulfilment of Jung's description
of what a psychically balanced and integrated religion of the
future might look like: "The union of the spiritual, masculine
principle with the feminine, psychic principle is far from being
just a fantasy of the Gnostics: it has found an echo in the Assumption of the Virgin, in the union of Tifereth and Malchuth,
and in Goethe's 'the Eternal Feminine leads up upwards and
on.'"[6] or "Logos and Eros are reunited, as if they had overcome
the conflict between spirit and flesh. They appear to know the
solution."[7]

In her thesis, Elaine reflects and comments on the ramifica-
tions of this psychic paradigm shift – incredibly – without hav-

3   See Erich Neumann, *The Great Mother: An Analysis of the Archetype*
(Princeton), and *The Origins and History of Consciousness* (Princeton).

4   Crowley, *The Equinox of the Gods* (New Falcon/OTO, 1991), p.134.

5   Crowley, *The Book of Thoth*, (Weiser, 1981), page 113.

6   Jung, *Mysterium Coniunctionis* (Collected Works of C. G. Jung Vol. 14,
Princeton, 1977), page 244.

7   Jung, *The Red Book: Liber Novus*, Appendix B, page 368.

ing "intellectual" access to the writings of Thelema until much later in her life. Her personal, individual efforts to emancipate the Self, stand as but one fractal of the Universal project of the complete emancipation of the human race. Elaine was singularly attuned to the treasure house of images that lie beneath the waking conscious, and by persistent effort, opened her heart to receive direct transmission from the collective unconscious of humankind. Many of her private revelations bear a startling resemblance to those found in the Holy Books of Thelema:

"The cross moves with me hanging on. I come to a big mirror, I see my guide - I'm on the ground now – I look up and see the face of a Greek-god-type young man with little curls - he comes toward me and we kiss."

Descent from the Cross

First falls the silly world; the world of the old grey land.
Falls it unthinkably far, with its sorrowful bearded face presiding over it; it fades to silence and woe.
We to silence and bliss, and the face is the laughing face of Eros.

Liber VII; 5:24-28

Here the cross of suffering and the sorrowful bearded face of the sufferer are transformed into the laughing face of Eros, or as Elaine comments "the petrification of the patriarchal animus is resolved and humanized through Eros-relatedness". Further, the "Black Madonna" revelation in her thesis, is an encounter with Babalon, the once-maligned "abominable" figure of the Christian apocalypse who "is sent as a redeemer to them that are below" in the system of Thelema. When Elaine writes "she is available to others but not lost in them" she is writing about one of the most sacred formulas of redemption in the new Aeon, and the *enantiodromia* of the divine feminine in human consciousness. It's unnecessary to relate every occasion where these remarkable resonances occur, but it's enough to say that Elaine's discovery of Thelema was a great comfort to her in her final years. She remarked to me that she finally had many of the answers she had sought throughout her life. Her only regret was that she didn't learn them sooner.

During one of my visits with her when she was first hospitalized, as she closed her eyes to better absorb what I was saying, I read her the Gnostic Mass - a central rite of Thelema that restores the role of the Priestess to the sacramental Mass. The level of concentration involved was intense. She trembled in ecstasy throughout. At one point, during the section of the Mass called 'Of the Office of the Collects, which are Eleven in Number', she gripped my hand and said "Say it again":

> Unto them from whose eyes the veil of life hath fallen may there be granted the accomplishment of their True Wills; whether they will absorption in the Infinite, or to be united with their chosen and preferred, or to be in contemplation, or to be at peace, or to achieve the labour and heroism of incarnation on this planet or another, or in any Star, or aught else, unto them may there be granted the accomplishment of their Wills; yea, the accomplishment of their Wills.

After which she joined me in intoning the response (which occurs throughout 'The Collects'):

"So mote it be."

Her work is a singular testament to the courage and fortitude of a woman determined to heal herself and the world around her: To take the leaden, lifeless images of a draconian 'pious' upbringing and transform these into spiritual gold. With this book, it is my great hope that her work continues to inspire others to do likewise.

So mote it be.

BRENDAN WALLS
Glen Huon, Tasmania
February, 2024

List of Figures and Plates

ILLUSTRATIONS

FIGURE 1. a. DIAGRAM OF A SUN WHEEL. b. DIAGRAM OF HAN MIRROR. From J.W. Perry, The Self in Psychotic Process, p. 84.

FIGURE 2. EMBLEM OF AKKADIAN SUN-GOD. From a model of the statue of Shamash in temple Ebarra in Sippar, 1913 B.C. (From Langdon, The Mythology of All Races.) ref. p. 30.

FIGURE 3. EMBLEM OF AKKADIAN SKY-GOD. Ideogram of ANU. (From Goblet D'Alviella, The Migration of Symbols.) ref. p. 30.

FIGURE 4. SUN WHEELS. a. MYCENAEN. From golden ornaments excavated from graves. (From Simpson, The Buddhist Praying Wheel.) b. Greek. From the emblem of the chariot of Apollo. (From Inman, Ancient Pagan and Modern Christian Symbolism.) ref. p. 30.

FIGURE 5. SUN WHEELS. a. Swiss lake dwellers. An amulet to which small charms were attached. b. Gallic. an altar from Clarensac, with sun wheel and thunderbolt. (Both from Simpson, The Buddhist Praying Wheel.) ref. p. 30.

FIGURE 6. SUN WHEELS. a. Dakotas (From Hastings, Encyclopedia of Religion and Ethics.) b. Mississippi. Engraved shell from the Mississippi mounds. (From Goblet D'Alviella, The Migration of Symbols.) ref. p. 30.

FIGURE 7. THE NOMMO-DOGON. (From Stewart, "Our Father who Art in Water," Simply Living, Australia, 1980.) ref. p. 56.

FIGURE 8. OANNES (2) and VISHNU. (From Stewart, "Our Father who Art in Water," Simply Living, Australia, 1980.) ref. p. 56.

FIGURE 9. EROS RIDING A DOLPHIN. (From Stewart, "Our Father who Art in Water," Simply Living, Australia, 1980.) ref. p. 57.

PLATES

PLATE I. QUADRATED CIRCLE AS COSMIC AXIS. Ceiling mandala of Tibetan Buddhism. (From Cammann, "Suggested Origin of the Tibetan Mandala Paintings." Art Quarterly, Spring, 1950, p. 107.)

PLATE II. MOUND BUILDER CROSS INSCRIBED ON SHELL. (Collection of Elaine (Simard) LaForêt) ref. p. 30.

PLATE III. EVEN-ARMED CROSS. (Collection of Elaine S. La-Forêt)

PLATE IV. RESURRECTION CROSS. Pine Driftwood from a Colorado lake. (Found by Elaine S. LaForêt) ref. p. 34.

PLATE V. COSMIC DIAGRAM. The transforming substance of European nature philosophy. (From Jung, Psychologie and Alchemie, Zurich, 1944.)

PLATE VI. ELF CROSS OF NATURE. (found by Elaine LaForêt) ref. p. 34.

PLATE VII. BIRD CROSS -IN FLIGHT. Wethered wood configuration from Heron Lake, New Mexico. (found by Elaine S. LaForêt) ref. p. 34.

PLATE VIII. NATARAJA. Cosmic dance of Hindu god Shiva. (bronze reproduction) ref. pp. 34, 36.

PLATE IX. CORN MANDALA. Painting by Diana Bryer. ref. p. 34.

PLATE X. DREAM IMAGE OF STANDING DOLPHIN-FISH IN REED BASKET. (Photographer Elaine LaForêt) ref. p. 25.

PLATE XI. DANCING TURTLE. Wood carving by Doug Hyde. (collection of Elaine LaForêt) ref. p. 43.

PLATES XII, XIII. BLACK MADONNA OF ROCAMADOUR. Virgin and Christ child from Rocamadour, Dordogne, France. ref. p. 49.

PLATE XIV. KARNAK SEKHMET. Black granite goddess sculpture in her temple at Karnak, Egypt. (photographer Peter Felsenthal) ref. pp. 49, 50, 51.

Bibliography

Allione, Tsultrim. *Women of Wisdom*, Routledge & Kegan Paul, Boston, MA, 1984.

Bachofen, Johann. *Myth, Religions and Mother Right*, New York: Bollingen Foundation, 1967.

Bradway, Katherine. *Villa of Mysteries*, C.G. Jung Institute of San Francisco, CA 1982.

Brooke Medicine Eagle. *Buffalo Woman Comes Singing*, Ballantine Books, NY, 1991.

Capra, Fritzjof. *Tao of Physics*, Shambala, Boston, 1991.

Clark, R.T. Rundle. *Myth and Symbol in Ancient Egypt*, Thames & Hudson, England, 1978.

Cory, Isaac Preston, *Ancient Fragments*, London, 1832, quoted in Hall, Manly P., *The Secret Teachings of All Ages*, The Philosophical Research Society, Inc., Los Angeles, 1977, p. LXXXV.

Craighead, Meinrad. *The Litany of the Great River*, Paulist Press. NY, 1991.

Eaton, Terry. *Joy Before Night*, The Theosophical Publishing House, Wheaton, IL, 1988.

Eliot. T.S. *Four Quartets*, "Little Gidding," Faber & Faber, London. 1955.

Ellis, Normandi, trans. *Awakening Osiris: A New Translation of the Egyptian Book of the Dead*, Phanes Press, MI, 1988.

Fox, Matthew. *The Coming of the Cosmic Christ*, Harper &t KoW; San Francisco, CA, 1980.

Hamilton, Edith. *Mythology*, Mentor Books, NY, 1969.

Hammerschlag, Carl. *The Dancing Healers*, Harper & Row, San Francisco, CA, 1988.

Hastings, James. *Encyclopedia of Religion and Ethics, Vol. IV*, NY, 1911, pp. 322-399.

Hawthorne, Nathaniel. "The Birthmark." *The Complete Novels and Selected Tales*, The Modern Library, Random House, NY, 1937.

Hillerman, Tony, ed. *The Spell of New Mexico*, Lawrence, D.I., "New Mexico," University of New Mexico Press, Albuquerque, 1976, pp. 29-36.

Hillman, James. "Dionysus in Jung's Writings," *Facing the Gods*, Spring Publication, Inc., University of Texas, Dallas, 1980.

Hillman, James. "Peaks and Vales," *Puer Papers*, Spring Publications, University of Dallas, 1979.

Hillman, James. *The Myth of Analysis*, Harper Colophon Books, NY, 1978, pp. 11-116; 215-290.

Howell, Alice O. *Jungian Symbolism in Astrology*. The Theosophical Publishing House, Wheaton, IL, 1987.

Hunbatz Men. *Secrets of Mayan Science/Religion*. Bear & Company, Santa Fe, 1990.

Johnson, Robert. *Ecstasy*, Harper & Row, San Francisco, 1987.

Jung, Carl Gustav. *Alchemical Studies, Collected Works*. Vol 13, Bollingen Series XX, Princeton University Press, 1976. p. 272

Jung, C.G. *The Archetypes and the Collective Consciousness*, Vol. 9.1. Bollingen Series XX, Princeton University Press, 1977, pp. 75-150.

Jung, C.G. and Kerenyi, C. *Essays on a Science of Mythology*, Bollingen Series XXI, Princeton University Press, 1973, pp. 66-69; 101-155.

Kerenyi, C. *Dionysus*, Bollingen Series LXV 2, Princeton University Press, 1976.

Kirsch, Hildegard. "Reveries on Jung," *Professional Reports 2*, March, 1975: 1-14.

Kumar, Sehdev. *The Vision of Kabir* (Concord, Ontario, Canada: Alpha & Omega, 1984.

Lederer, Laura, ed. *Take Back The Night: Women on Pornography*; Lorde, Andre, "Uses of the Erotic: the Erotic as Power," NY, 1980.

Munro, Eleanor. *On Glory Roads*, Thames & Hudson, 1987.

Neumann, Erich. *The Great Mother*, Bollingen Series XLVI, Princeton University Press, 1974.

Perry, J.W. *The Self in Psychotic Process*, Spring Publications, Dallas, 1987.

Sams, Jamie, and David Carson, *Medicine Cards: The Discovery of Power Through the Ways of Animals*, Bear & Co., Santa Fe. 1988.

Schure, Edouard. *From Sphinx to Christ*, Harper & Row, San Francisco, 1970.

Stewart, David. "Our Father Who Art in Water," in *Simply Living. No 11, 12*, Australia, 1980, pp. 24-37; 60-70.

ABOUT THE AUTHOR

Elaine LaForet Allistone: Jungian Analyst and Scholar[1]

Nature and Human Nature

We are part of Nature. The work of our time is to repair damage done by humankind to the human connection to the Earth and all sentient beings: other humans, animals, plants, trees, stones........it is crucial that we, like Jung, remember THE EARTH HAS A SOUL: (The Nature Writings of C.G. Jung, ed. By Meredith Sabini, 2002.)

Born in the USA, Elaine has lived in New Jersey, New York, Massachusetts, Connecticut, and California. At 52 with three children grown, she resettled herself in Sante Fe, New Mexico, and began spending three months each year in Australia, particularly Tasmania, to write poetry and vignettes and to hike. In Tasmania, she communed with the trees, the sea and people living harmoniously and creatively close to Nature. She moved to northwest Tasmania and to Hobart in December 2002.

Elaine has travelled extensively and intensively throughout the world (Canada, Mexico, Japan, Taiwan, India, Nepal. Iran, Syria, Lebanon, Jordan, Israel, Turkey, Greece, Egypt, Scandinavia, France, Italy, Germany, Switzerland, England, Scotland, New Zealand and Fiji.) She has studied literature, world religions, art and the human psyche. Exploring outer worlds serves to ground her knowledge in experiences of actual places and people - - - in the landscape of the Planet itself.

Elaine connects through images and the heart --- wordless-

---

1   This biography was written by the author in 2012.

ly --- with her cat Lion, hummingbirds, dragonflies, turtles, trees, eagles, white wolves, bears, owls, squirrels, babies and other humans, stones, clouds, whales, dolphins, roses, rosemary, huntsman spiders, abalones, swallows, swans, snakes, sunflowers, cacti...... She observes and receives their responses with gratitude for kinship. She is deeply inspired by the Native American Peoples of the Southwest.

Elaine's thesis "Descent from the Cross: Transformation of a Masochistic Woman" marked the completion of her psychoanalytic degree at the C.G. Jung Institute of New York. She has practiced psychoanalysis for many years, taught at the C. G. Jung Institute of New Mexico, presented public lectures (one is entitled "The Symbol of the Cross: Revitalizing the Balanced Cross of Nature") and classes and workshops for the public. She has a BA from Wellesley College and an MA from Harvard University in literature, psychology and teaching.

Her desire to understand Human Nature, animals, spirituality, ancient wisdom and ways of life, and all of Nature persists. Healing modalities and the body-psyche-spirit interface claim much of her attention...

Every day she is greeted by the impulse of service to life in some way and with gratitude for Being and Beauty in its many forms right now. She has loved many, of many ages and species, and rejoices in an ever-widening extended family. Transforming worry and embracing the NOW fully is an ongoing challenge, as is patience and receptivity.

Poem

Untended inner natures

  grow weeds

   greed

Seeds of thought

  sprout unbidden

What is hidden

  seeks expression.

      a conscious mind

    Weed a hopeful heart

    Cultivate a faithful soul

LIVING IN THE SUNLIGHT

MAKING A FORGOTTEN MEDITATION AN ATOMIC HABIT

https://livinginthesunlight.site/

ISBN 978-0645103946

Living in the Sunlight by Steve King is a little gem of a book that is welcome and much needed, perhaps never as much as right now. Dedicated to the exposition of a deceptively simple meditation practice, the book's clear and unassuming narrative is brimful with initiated knowledge, and steeped in the esoteric lore of Ordo Templi Orientis and Aleister Crowley's Thelema. The practice of "Living in the Sunlight," however, originates not with Crowley but with his "scarlet woman" Hilarion (Jeanne Robert Foster) and can be adopted by anyone, irrespective of denominational affiliations and ideological convictions. In essence, it is a method of identifying one's deepest awareness with the Sun, for the ultimate purpose of radiating its light unto others. An antidote to the present culture of cynicism and ennui, Living in the Sunlight is based on a simple yet profound notion that happiness is contagious and grows by sharing. This book, and the method of putting it into practice, is rooted in a most radical idea, that the point of life is joy. Highly recommended.

- Gordan Djurdjevic, author of India and the Occult, and co-translator of Sayings of Gorakhnāth

THE LEGEND OF ALEISTER CROWLEY

https://thelegendofaleistercrowley.com/

ISBN 978-0645103939

This facsimile edition of P. R. Stephensen's 1930 broadside against the 'Campaign of Personal Vilification Unparalleled in Literary History' arrives in 2021 as the mainstream media thrashes in its death throes.

Quality digital scans of the original book, never before published material from the Australian OTO archives, as well as a new essay examining the politics of conspiracy and the pathologies of Fake News, make this an indispensable case study of media malfeasance and moral panic.

Currently available from In Perpetuity Publishing.

For more information about our publications please visit

https://www.otoaustralia.org.au/publications/

Available through all good online booksellers.

ORA ET LABORA

https://ora-et-labora.site/

Distributed across three volumes, wide-ranging and highly eclectic essays from around the world, *Ora Et Labora* gathers together the research and findings of the practitioner-scholars of Thelema.

VOL I
ISBN 978-0645103908

In the Weaves of the Order • Typology of Will in writings of Aleister Crowley, Meister Eckhart and Carl Gustav Jung • An Analysis of Liber Librae • When meditation goes bad • Health in Thelema: The Stone of the Wise & The Holy Guardian Angel • Eros daimon mediator and Electoral College • On the Epiclesis • Secret Light: Reflections on the Rosy Cross • Eucharist: From Self to God • The Proof is in the Pudding • Baphomet

VOL II
ISBN 978-0645103915

Ãmi Satya: Hallaj, Crowley, and the Baul Fakirs of Bengal • Carl Kellner • Freemasonry, the OTO, and Crowley • Aleister Crowley: a K2 Letter • The Spiritual Heritage from Egypt • Notes towards a preliminary analysis of a peculiar motif in the Stele of Ankh-af-na-khonsu • The Birth of the New Aeon: Magick And Mysticism of Thelema from the Perspective of Postmodern A/Theology • Crowley, Conspiracy, Moral Panic and the Media • The Will of the Aeon

Vol III
ISBN 978-0645103922

Alba ad Rubrum: Waratah Blossoms • Lord of Life & Joy • The 'Occult Macrohistory' of Aleister Crowley • Mundus Imaginalis, the Stone of the Wise • Bread and Salt: To be taken with a grain of salt • Initiation and the Hermetic Tradition • The mantras and the spells: Language and magick • "Anything can be Animated": The Visionary Cinema of Jordan Belson and its Esoteric Core • Occultists, Nazis, Atlanteans and Alawites. Vril and the Occult Revival • 'That I may follow and dispel the night': Wagner's Parsifal and Liber XV • A Crack in Everything : Finitude and the Ceremony of the Introit • An Examination of the Symbolism of the Gnostic Mass Temple • Temple Theology in the Gnostic Mass • Apokalypsis II: Temple mysticism in the New Aeon : An Introduction • The Island of Flames and the spiritual heart. A reflective commentary on Rev. Cosmé Hallelujah's "Notes towards a preliminary analysis of a peculiar motif in the Stele of Ankh-af-na-khonsu" • Excursus on Notes towards a preliminary analysis of a particular motif in the Stele of Ankh-af-na-khonsu

Vol IV
ISBN 978-06451039-7-7

The life of the Sun, the joy of the Earth: an orientation for practice and awareness in the M...M...M... • The Mythology of the Eucharist • The Solar Myth and The Path of Initiation • VIAOV: The Monomyth of Aleister Crowley • The Therion File • A World of Difference • The Left Hand Path • Liber Samekh • The Konami Code: Crowley, card games and the occult • The Birth of Hell: Formulae of Initiation in The Book of Two Ways and the Ceremony of the Death of Asar • Reading

BD Spell 30: the mindful heart of Ankh-ef-en-khonsu • Apo-kalypsis III: Depth Revelation • Introduction to Larry Sitsky's Music (piano and chorus) for Ecclesiae Gnosticae Catholicae Canon Missae • Music (piano and chorus) for Ecclesiae Gnosticae Catholicae Canon Missae

THE BEST OF OZ

https://thebestofoz.com/

After 13 years and 50 Issues, OTO Grand Lodge of Australia is making its member-only OZ magazine available to the public in this 'best of' compilation. Inspiring and provocative, OZ chronicles the birth and early development of the Australian Grand Lodge experiment in thought leadership, scholarship, culture and magical design.

ISBN 978-0646815770

Origins of the modern O.T.O in Australia • Aurora Australis: topological reflections on the modern M.M.M. in Australia • 'New Commentary' Theology: Notes towards reorganising the EGC Part 1 & Part 2 • 'From the GM' (AUGL in Japan) • Toiling in the (local) fields of Our Lord • Remembering Parsi Krumm-Heller (1925-2008 e.v.) Obituary • Grand Master Shiva's Introduction to J. Daniel Gunther's 'Initiation in the Aeon of the Child: the Path of the Great Return' • Veni Cooper-Mathieson • Woman Girt with a Sword • EGC Retreat Keynote Address • Our Church – the Clarity of Vocation • Shadow of the Thelemites: the Abbot, the Abbey and the Nightmare • In the Flesh – Manifesting Liber 194 • Battle of the Ants • Apokalypsis 418 – The Temple of Christ, the Angelic priesthood and the Great Return of the Queen of Heaven • Temple Mount: The Oriental Templar crusade for Verità • Living In The Sunlight

www.ingramcontent.com/pod-product-compliance
Lightning Source LLC
Chambersburg PA
CBHW060043030426

42334CB00019B/2460